Fairs and Revels

Fairs and Revels

Brian Jewell

MIDAS BOOKS

In the same illustrated series

Victorians on the Thames, Reginald Bolland
Spas and Watering Places, Muriel Searle
Sports and Games, Brian Jewell
The Working Travellers, Brian Jewell (in preparation)
Bathing Machines and Bloomers, Muriel Searle (in preparation)
Nation of Shopkeepers, Brian Jewell (in preparation)
Circuses and Menageries, Brian Jewell (in preparation)

First published 1976 by
MIDAS BOOKS
12 Dene Way, Speldhurst,
Tunbridge Wells, Kent TN3 0NX

© Brian Jewell 1976
Designed by David Morley-Clarke

ISBN 0 85936 068 7

Printed in Great Britain
by Chapel River Press, Andover, Hants.

Contents

Cover/Jacket: *Peasant Dance* by Brueghel (c. 1525/30-1569)
Endpapers: *An English Merry Making in the Olden Time* Art Union
of London 1852. Engraved by William Holl. Painted by
T. W. R. Frith ARA

The Bartholomew Fair

In fifty-five, may I never thrive,
  If I tell you any more than is true.
In London she came, hearing of fame
  Of a fair called Bartholomew.

In houses of boards, men walk upon cords,
  As easy as squirrels crack filberds;
But the cut-purses they do lite, and rub away,
  But these we suppose to be ill birds.

For a penny you may see a fine puppet play,
  And for two-pence a rare piece of art;
And a penny a cann, I dare swear a man,
  May put six of 'em into a quart.

Their sights are so rich, is able to bewitch
  The heart of a very fine man-a;
Here's patient Grizel here and fair Rosamond there,
  And the history of Susana.

At Pye-corner end, mark well, my good friend,
  'tis a very fine dirty place;
Where there's more arrows and bows, the Lord above knows,
  Than there was handl'd at Civy Chase.

Then at Smithfield Bars, betwixt the ground and the stars,
  There's a place they call Shoemaker Row,
Where that you may buy shoes every-day,
  Or go barefoot all the year I too.

The Song of the Bartholomew Fair.

Author's Note

This is a book concerned with British fairs, revels, festivals, feasts and wakes—all communal gatherings for the purpose of merrymaking.

All civilisations have recognised the need for revitalisation through pleasure. In Rome, festivals were based either on civil occasions, anniversaries of military victories, celebrations of rulers' birthdays or religious commemorations; there were so many that one may wonder how they found time to do anything else.

The British drew their reasons to make merry from the many sources which had influence on these islands: the cultures of the Celts, the Romans, the Norse and the Normans, as well as creating a few of their own.

Looking back on the revels of the past brings a suspicion that we may have lost the art of having fun. However village fêtes still survive as a means of fund-raising for various charities, the travelling showmen's fairs are alive and well, and the most recent form of fair, the steam engine rally—with its nostalgic reminder of the not too distant past—is a welcome newcomer.

Brenda Kidman, an authority on today's showmen, has given an excellent sketch of the activities and problems of these magnificent people in her Epilogue to the book. The showman has a lineage of tradition which is, some would claim and I subscribe to this point of view, rivalled only by that of the innkeeper. Long may he flourish in this increasingly automated and computorised world.

I am grateful for the chance of outlining the way our ancestors enjoyed themselves and hope that the book may go some way towards showing what a revel should be about—having fun.

Tunbridge Wells, July, 1976.   *B.J.*

1. Market Fairs

Commerce was the parent of the great fairs, originally markets and mostly established by the grant of Royal Charter under which they could be set up only on certain days of the year, or between specified dates. The boundaries of the fair were also defined, and the security of the merchants, not only during the period of the fair but while journeying to and from it, was guaranteed. As a sign of this protection, a large stuffed glove was displayed on a pole carried in procession and later at the gates of the town.

The glove is up, let the fair begin.

Most of the English Charter Fairs had their origins in Norman and subsequent times but it is known that markets of this kind were held much earlier, going back to the days of the Roman Empire. The name itself, *fair*, is derived from the Latin, *feria*, meaning a holiday.

One of the most ancient of the English markets was the St Giles Hill Fair near Winchester, instituted in the time of William the Conqueror as a revenue raiser for the Bishop of Winchester.

Unlawful traders at St Giles Hill, who plied their trades within the jurisdiction of the fair while it was in progress—an area extending as far as Southampton—forfeited their goods to the Bishop.

At sunrise, the members of the Bishop's Pavilion Court received the keys of the city from the Mayor and Bailiff. For the next sixteen days the fair's own Mayor and Bailiff held power, administering justice to all offenders in Winchester and Southampton and in the surrounding district known as the *seven league circuit*.

The right to hold a fair was a highly prized privilege. Tolls were permitted to be charged on all goods bought and sold, which was a valuable asset for the patentees. At the Midsummer Fair at Chester—basically a wool trading and animal market—the toll imposed by the Abbot was four pence for every sack of wool sold, and a like sum for every three pigs.

Charters were not easily obtained, granted only when protective regulations and restrictions could be guaranteed by the landowners, religious establishments and the towns and villages themselves.

Valentine

Although in this book we are mainly concerned with gatherings

9

in the British Isles, mention must also be made of the great fairs abroad. In the Champagne district of 12th century France, there were six main fairs that extended over the whole year. Among these were the fairs of Provins and Troyes, the latter giving its name to the internationally accepted *troy* weight standard. The Leipzig Fair was famous as a market for leather, cloth and furs. Hungary had its great fair at Pesth; Italy had the Bergamo, while Nijni-Novrorod in Russia, and Kiakhta in Siberia were the fairs where the products of East and West were exchanged.

Some fairs, mainly those with their origins in Church Wakes, were set up without a charter. In time they achieved equal status with the charter fairs and were granted this patent.

Almost without exception, the market fairs have degenerated into purely pleasure fairs, and would not have survived without the support of travelling showmen.

A fair would often open with a 'riding'. For instance, at the village of Avingham (sometime called Abingham), now Oving-ham, on the river Tyne, the twice-yearly fair started with a procession from the village ale-house, accompanied by two Northumberland pipers.

An 18th century diarist wrote of the Avingham Fair:

Anglo-Saxon Gleemen

A 13th century tumbler

After baking sufficient number of barley bannocks for the following day and milk set up, they throw off their linsey-woolsey petticoats and hale-made bed-goons, a good specimen of their taste, in the two warmest colours, a red flower or stripe upon a yellow ground, and as much of a third colour round the waist, as would make them vie with Iris. In this butterfly state they hasten to the scene of mirth, and most of them dance till they have reason to suppose it time to 'gang home', and git a ready be crowdie time.

The day following the fair at Avingham was known as Gwonny Jokesane's Day (Granny Jackson's Day), recalling some otherwise long-forgotten character. A leader, who the villagers called 'the mayor' was elected and, sat in a litter, carried to the minister's house, where this speech was made:

A yes! Twa times yes! If ony man, or ony man's man, lairds, loons, lubberdoons, dogs, skelpers, gabbrigate swingers, shall commit a parliament as a twarliament, we, in the township o' Avingham, shall hea his legs, his heed, tied ta tha cagwheel, till he say yence, twice prosper the fair o' Avingham an' Gwonny Jokesane's Day.

Everyone cheered and there followed drinking at the manse and dancing outside, accompanied by the Northumberland pipers.

10

Utrecht Fair

The 'mayor' was then remounted in his litter and the parade proceeded to other houses where they were likely to be welcomed with similar hospitality.

All fairs had their peculiarities. In the 18th century the people of Brough used to put up the contents of their gardens in a lottery at the time of the fair, a penny being the price of a ticket. Many specialised in the sale of a particular class of commodity. At Dewsbury there was the Onion Fair where children sang:

Onion Fair, Onion Fair,
if you don't let us have a holiday
We'll all run away.

Horses were sold at Grantham under a charter granted in 1463. In the reign of Richard III the charter was improved to include a prison and to hold two annual fairs.

11

The York Dish Fair was so called because of the small domestic
wares sold there. It was held on St Luke's Day under a charter
granted by Henry VII. The fair opened with a procession headed
by four men carrying a large ladel slung between them.

For most people the first specialised fair that comes to mind is
the Nottingham Goose Fair. There was a market at Nottingham
from Saxon times, but it was not until 1284 that a charter was
granted by Edward I for a fair to last fifteen days each year. In
addition, there was an eight day fair on or about the Feast of
St Matthew (21 September). It is this latter fair that has survived
as the Goose Fair, the largest trading gathering in the Midlands.

The name Goose Fair first appears in a 1542 record of a purchase by John Trussell, steward of the Willoughby family of
Woolaton. In the following year, 1543, there was a demand from
the Sheriffs of Nottingham for an allowance of one shilling and
eight pence in respect of twenty-two stalls on Goose Fair Day.

The Goose Fair was held at the time of the year when geese
are in their prime: roast goose was the traditional dish in England
at Michaelmas (29 September) in a like way that turkey has been
eaten at Christmas for the past century. Twenty thousand and
more geese were brought to the fair 'on foot' from farms in
Lincolnshire and Norfolk, their feet being treated with tar and
sand in preparation for the journey.

One of the more spectacular moments in the history of the
Nottingham Goose Fair occurred in 1766—the year of the
'Cheese Riot', when the public, enraged by high prices, hurled

March Fair at Brough

cheeses at the stallholders. During the course of the uprising the mayor suffered the indignity of being bowled over.

The original fifteen days of the fair were reduced to five in 1876, and to three in 1880, about the time when the showman's part of the festivities began to replace the trading role.

Another Goose Fair, or rather 'Goosey Fair' as it was called in this case, was held at Tavistock.

The number of market fairs in England diminished after the time of Edward I, but many continued, among them the Stourbridge Fair in Cambridgeshire, said to have originated from a grant from King John to the leper hospital at Stourbridge (Stowbridge, Sturbitch or Stirbitch). A charter was given by Henry VIII to the magistrate and corporation of Cambridge for the fair to be opened for a fortnight after 19 September.

13

Stourbridge Fair Booth

William Hone, quoting from *Privileges of the University of Cambridge* by George Dyer, again quoting from an earlier work by Fuller, on the origin of the Stourbridge Fair, states that about the year 1417, a clothier from Kendal on his way to London, washed his cloth in the river and offered it for sale at a reduced price. The following year he brought more cloth to the same place and subsequently more traders came to Stourbridge to make the market an annual event.

According to the charter, if the corn on the field was not cut by 24 August, the fair builders were allowed to tread it down. On the other hand, if the fair was not cleared by noon on Michaelmas Day, the farmers may come in and destroy what remained. The field in which the fair was held was about half a mile square and about two miles from Cambridge market, the river Cam running to the north side and the Stour to the East. In this area were built rows of shops and booths, and in a few cases, brick buildings. The 'roads' were given names which were retained each year: Garlick Row, Bookseller's Row, Cook Row, etc.,

14

where the traders plied their wares—goldsmiths, toymen, braziers, turners, milliners, haberdashers, hatters, mercers, drapers, china warehousemen, tavern keepers, keepers of coffee houses and eating places, many of the traders coming from as far as Germany, Italy and France.

The principal commodities of the Stourbridge Fair were butter and cheese, hops and wool. In the *duddery* alone, upwards of £100,000 worth of woollen goods were sold. But, like the Bartholomew Fair in London, it was also an occasion for entertainment, with horse racing and the usual revel-type games as attractions. The sideshows featured plays, drolls and music, and rope dancing.

By 1613, according to Drake's *Shakespeare and His Times*, the fair had become the largest in England, and was so popular that it attracted hackney carriages from as far afield as London.

London had more than its share of fairs. By 1825, the Deptford Fair was a considerable event, with sports, games, dancing and drinking booths. The pleasure side of the fair is said to have originated as a diversion among those who assembled to see the Master and Brothers of Trinity House (incorporated 1514) on their annual visit to Deptford. At first few games were played, jingling matches and the like, but gradually the booth keepers and the showmen came in abundance.

The July Fair on Highgate Green was centred on The Flask, a tavern built in the reign of Henry VI which, by the way, was a favourite drinking and resting place of the highwayman, Dick Turpin.

At one time called 'Our Lady's Fair', the Southwark Fair used to be opened by the Lord Mayor of London attended by the Sheriffs. Evelyn, in his diary (1660), records seeing a rope-walking monkey at the fair who 'turned heels over head with a basket having eggs in it without breaking any'.

There is a legend of King John killing a stag at Peckham—now a district of South East London—and so enjoying the day's sport that he granted a charter to hold an annual fair. Be that as it may, it seems likely that by 1279 a fair was being held at Camberwell, for it was in that year that Gilbert de Clare was summoned before John of Ryegate and other justices to show by what right he claimed privilege of holding assize of ale and bread in his village of Camberwell. The Camberwell Fair, specialising in booths selling 'good drinks, pyes and pedlerie trash' lasting for three weeks, continued as an annual August event until well into the late 19th century.

The most important of the London revels was the Bartholomew Fair. About the year 1102, in the reign of Henry I, the priory, church and hospital of St Bartholomew was founded by one,

Plan of Stourbridge Fair

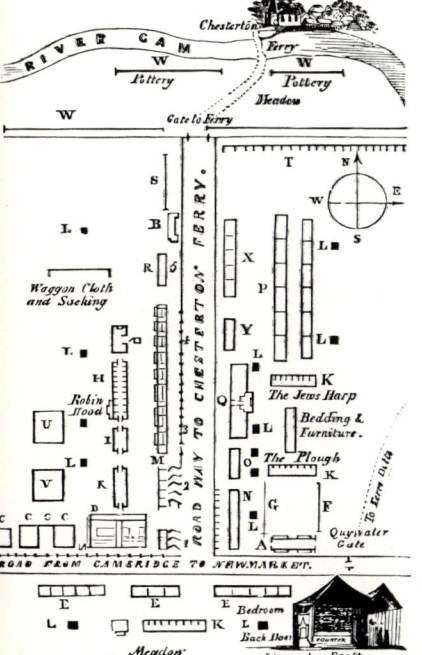

Rahere, a minstrel of the king, after a pilgrimage to Rome where St Bartholomew is reputed to have appeared to him with instructions to establish a priory in the district known as Smithfield—near the tournament and jousting field, which is still recalled by such road names as Giltspur Street and Knightrider Street. Rahere was somehow able to raise the money to establish his complex of buildings and become the first prior.

Henry II granted to the priory a charter to hold the Bartholomew Fair annually for the benefit of clothiers and drapers. In subsequent centuries, until the Commonwealth put a stop to fairs and other forms of entertainment, the Bartholomew and Stourbridge Fairs were the two great markets of England. The fair in Smithfield was held in early September, although there is a reference to 24 August as the opening day in 1641.

Bartholomew Fair

Morris Dancers

According to Ben Jonson, the Fair in 1614 included such varied attractions as a tooth drawer, wrestling and shooting games, a whipping post, and a 'juggler with a well educated ape to come over the chain for the King of England and back again for the prince and to sit on his hindquarters for the Pope and the king of Spain'.

Ninety-five years, a Commonwealth and a Restoration of the Monarchy later, Ned Ward in *London Spy* tells of a visit to the Bartholomew Fair:

Harper and Hoppestrere

We ordered the coachman to set us down at the Hospital gate near which he went into a convenient house to smoke a pipe, and overlook the follies of the innumerable throng, whose impatient desires of seeing Merry Andrew's grimaces, had led them ankle deep into filth and nastiness. The first objects, when we were seated at the window that lay within our observation were the quality of the Fair, strutting round their balconies in their tinsey robes, and golden leather buckskins.

By the early 19th century this was the only fair held within the bounds of the City of London. The proceedings opened with a Lord Mayor's procession from the Mansion House to Smithfield where a proclamation was read by an attorney and repeated by an officer of the Sheriff. The procession then returned to the Mansion House, via Newgate.

There can be no doubt that, like most market gatherings, the

17

On previous page
Flemish Fair
Pieter Brueghel
The Younger, 1564

Bartholomew Fair was a place for rowdy merrymaking. Many attempts were made to bring about a ban but it continued until 1885.

The Smithfield event was not England's sole Bartholomew Fair. Another was held at Newbury, Berkshire, lasting two days, and established under a charter granted by King John. It was at Newbury, up to the beginning of the 19th century, that there used to be practised the mock election of the 'Mayor of Bartle-mas', followed by a feast of bacon and beans. The celebration included a procession with the *mayor* carrying a mace comprising a cabbage at the end of a pole.

Many fairs have vanished, having no place in what we like to call *modern* life. Where they have survived, the nature has changed, No longer is a fair a great market—commerce is just not carried on in this way any longer—pleasure is the principal function of all fairs in the 20th century. But let us not forget one type of event which still has an element of the fairs of old—the international exhibitions of trade and industry. The interpretation of the word *fair* may have changed but old habits die hard.

Gentry playing a fashionable game of the time

20

2. Hirings and Mops

The first employment exchanges were the gatherings known as Hirings, Mops or Statutes (Stattits).

The word *mop* for a hiring fair was probably derived from the fashion for girls to carry mops as an indication that they were available for hire as domestic servants. Standing in rows, the applicants awaited a new employer. Naturally, such gatherings attracted food and drink sellers, thus making a basis for a full-scale unchartered fair.

The terms under which a master could employ a servant and the wages that had to be paid were first regulated by an Act of 1351 necessitated by the acute shortage of labour that followed the plague of 1347–9. This law called for every able-bodied man to offer himself for hire. Justices of each county met at *Statute Sessions* once a year between Easter and Michaelmas and the mop fairs usually followed the sittings of these courts. Further strengthening of labour laws was brought in by an Act of 1563.

By law, the contracts made at hiring fairs were for one year but in practice it was only for fifty-one weeks. The object of this lost week was to avoid paying parish benefit if the worker should become unemployed and fall upon hard times—not that everyday life was particularly easy! It was customary to pay benefits only if the recipient was in regular employment within the parish for a period not less than one year. The contract was ratified by the new master giving the worker a token of *earnest money*, also known as the *hiring money, God's penny* or *fasten penny*. If the servant was found to be inefficient or of bad character before taking up his employment, the master would tell him to 'go and drink his earnest money'. Alternatively, a servant who changed his mind or found a better master could give up the job by returning his earnest money. By the 19th century the penny had inflated twelve-fold to one shilling.

If a servant found himself, or herself, unemployed after a hiring fair it was possible to have a second chance at what was called a *Runaway Mop*—a fair usually held about a fortnight after the main Mop Fair. Such a runaway was the St Luke's Fair at Henley-in-Arden.

The Mops were important days in the normally dull lives of

Two Revelling Figures

the servants, relieved only by the charter fairs in towns and the parish wakes. Inevitably they sought all manner of recreation and entertainment. After the serious business of employment had been settled, the Mop Fair became something of a marriage market, naturally with a liberal amount of celebration in the traditional manner at the tavern. By the middle of the 19th century feelings were running high against these 'drunken affairs' which resulted in the establishment of 'Servants' Registration Offices' where the exchange of labour could be performed with more decorum. This was followed in 1909 by the foundation of Labour Exchanges and from then on the Mop Fairs existed in name only.

A description of a Mop Fair at Studley, Warwickshire, is given by a correspondent to the *Table Book* (1827):

On arriving, between twelve and one o'clock, at the part of the Alcester Road where the assembly was held, the place was filling very fast by groups of persons of almost every descriptions from every quarter. Towards three o'clock there must have been many thousands present. The appearance of the whole way be pretty accurately portrayed to the mind of those who have witnessed a country fair; the sides of the road were occupied with stalls for gingerbread, cakes, etc., general assortments of hardware, japanned goods, waggoner's frocks, and an endless variety of wearing apparel, suitable to every class, from the farm bailiff, or dapper footman, to the unassuming ploughboy, or day-labourer.

The public houses were full, not excepting even the private chambers. The scene out of doors was enlivened, here and there by some wandering minstrel, or fiddler, round whom stood a crowd of men and boys, who, at intervals, eagerly joined to swell the chorus of the song. Although there was as large an assemblage as could be well remembered, both of masters and servants, I was given to understand that there was very little hiring. This might happen from a twofold cause;

Hiring Fair at Burford

Hiring Servants

first, on account of its being one of the early Statutes, and, secondly, from the circumstances of the servants asking what was deemed (considering the pressure of the times) exorbitant wages. The servants were, for the most part, bedecked in their best church-going clothes. The men also wore clean white frocks and carried in their hats some emblem or insignia of the situation they had been accustomed to or were desirous to fill: for instance, a waggoner, or ploughboy, had a piece of whipcord in his hat, some of it ingeniously plaited in a variety of ways and entwined round the hatband; a cowman, after the same manner, had some cow-hair; and to those already mentioned there was occasionally added a piece of sponge; a shepherd had wool; a gardener had flowers, etc.

The girls wishing to be hired were in a spot apart from the men and boys, and all stood not unlike cattle at a fair waiting for dealers. Some of them held their hands before them, with one knee protruding (like soldiers standing at ease), and never spoke save when catechised and examined by a master or mistress as to the work they had been

23

accustomed to; and then you would scarce suppose they had learned to say anything but 'Ees, sur', or 'No, sur', for these were almost the only expressions that fell from their lips. Others, on the contrary, exercised no small degree of self-sufficient loquacity concerning their abilities, which not unusually consisted of a good proportion of main strength, or being able to drive or follow a variety of kinds of plough. Where a master or mistress was engaged in conversation with a servant they were usually surrounded by a group, with their mouths extended to an angle of nearly forty-five degrees, as if to catch the sounds at the aperture; this in some, perhaps, was mere idle curiosity, in others, from desire to know the wages asked and given, as a guide for themselves. I observed a seeming indifference about the servants in securing situations. They appeared to require a certain sum for wages, without reference to any combination of circumstances or the state of the times . . .

When a bargain is concluded on at a 'Statute', it is the custom to ratify it immediately, and on the spot, by the master presenting the servant what is termed 'earnest money', which is usually one shilling, but it varies according to circumstances; for instance, if a servant agrees to come for less than he at first asked, it is, perhaps, on the condition that his earnest is augmented, probably doubled or trebled, as may be agreed upon . . .

When the hiring is over, the emblems in the hats are exchanged for ribbons of almost every hue. Some retire to the neighbouring grounds to have games at bowls, skittles, or pitching, etc., whilst the more

Burlesque Music

24

unwary are fleeced of their money by the itinerant Greeks and black legs with E.O.* tables, pricking in the garter, and the three thimbles, etc. These tricksters seldom fail to reap abundant harvests at the Statutes. Towards evening each lad seeks his lass, and they hurry off to spend the night at the public-houses, or, as is the case in some small villages, at private houses, which are licensed on these occasions.

* The E-O (Even-Odd) gaming wheel was introduced in about 1740 at the Assembly Rooms at Tunbridge Wells, and developed from the *hoca* wheels used at Saint-Cyr, Baden-Baden, Baden-bei-Wien, and Pest. These were the games on which roulette were founded. E-O, or *roly-poly* comprised a wheel with forty compartments, twenty of which were marked 'E' and the others marked 'O'. If the ball landed in an 'E' compartment, the banker took all the stakes on 'O' and vice versa. It was a popular game with the ladies taking the spa waters and was actually prescribed by one of the doctors of the town: 'of a morning and post-noon, the waters; and in the evening the excitement of the Roly-Poly tables; watching which brings out the vapours'.

E & O Gambling Game

Top: A Fools Dance
Below: Morris Dancers

To attempt to delineate the scenes that now present themselves, would on my part be presumption indeed. It rather requires the pencil of Hogarth to do justice to the varied picture. Here go round the

'Song and dance, and mirth and glee'

but I cannot add, with the poet,

'In one continued round of harmony'.

for, among such a mingled mass, it is rare but that in some part discord breaks in upon the public amusements of the peaceable inclined. The rooms of the several houses are literally crammed, and usually remain so throughout the night, unless they happen to be under restrictions from the magistrates, in which case the houses are

26

shut at a stated hour, or the license risked. Clearances, however, are not easily effected. At a village not far from hence, it has ere now, been found necessary to disturb the reverend magistrate from his peaceful slumbers, and require his presence to quell disturbances that almost, as natural consequences ensue, from the landlords and proprietors of the houses attempting to turn out guests, who, under the influence of liquor, pay little regard to either landlord or magistrate. The most peaceable way of dealing, is to allow them to remain till dawn breaks in and warns them home.

In regard to the licensing of private houses, it must be remembered that outside the cities at that time, a very large proportion of ale was brewed domestically and consumed at home. It was the more enterprising of these home brewers who, with the approval of the magistrates, opened their doors and turned publicans for the period of the fair.

Among the many Statutes or Mop Fairs throughout Britain were those held at Stratford-upon-Avon; Southaw, Warwickshire; Shipston-on-Stour, Warwickshire; Aston Cantlow, Warwickshire; Studley and Henley-in-Arden.

Daily hirings can hardly be considered as fairs or celebrations but the fact remains that when workers gathered in the mornings in the hope of gaining employment, the atmosphere was something of a festive occasion. In London the traditional places for these gatherings between 5 and 6 o'clock in the morning, were Cheapside and Charing Cross.

Acrobats and Tumblers

3. Wakes and Saints' Feast Days

Wakes were the parish celebrations. They were held either on the anniversary of the consecration of a particular church or on the Feast Day of the Saint to whom the church was dedicated. Apart from the religious services, the parishioners took the chance of enjoying themselves and traders the opportunity of business, setting up stalls in the churchyard and often in the church itself. Wakes often developed into full-scale market fairs and some were eventually granted royal charters.

The word *wake* was applied to this form of festivity because originally the parishioners fasted and stayed awake in the church on the eve of the day in question.

After the Reformation the religious aspects of Wakes and Saints' Days declined and more emphasis was placed on merry-making, resulting in rowdiness and drunken behaviour. The popularity of Wakes diminished as pastimes became more genteel, and died out almost completely in the middle years of the 19th century.

St Bartholomew is the patron saint of the church at Westhoughton, Lancashire, where the Feast Day (24 August) marks the start of the town's Wakes Week. In years gone by there used to be baked a large communal pie in the shape of a cow's head— the Westhoughton people are still affectionately known as cowheads in the surrounding district.

St James's Feast Day (25 July) has a connection with sheep. This was the day of the Ebernoe Horn Fair in Sussex, at which a horned sheep was roasted whole. After cooking, the carcass was decapitated and the head given to the winning team of a cricket match, to be mounted on the wall of the local pub.

A singed sheep's head also played a part in St Andrew's Day celebrations on 30 November. It was carried in procession through the streets of London by the Scots. A sheep's head, duly singed, seems to have had some significance at Duddingston, Edinburgh where, up to the early 19th century, it was considered a delicacy.

Lamb or mutton may have constituted the feasts for some saints but Michaelmas (29 September) has roast goose as the traditional

Mystery or Miracle Play

29

St Patrick's Day

table dish, in the same way as it is now the custom to have roast turkey at Christmas.

'Church Ales' were held on St John the Baptist Day (24 July) at Elverton and Okebroke, Derbyshire, at which 'every husband and wife shall pay two pence and every cottager one penny'. Church Ales were popular entertainments in medieval, Tudor and Stewart times, particularly after the Reformation, as a means of fund raising. The church house and sometimes the church itself was taken over for the purpose. Here the church wardens sold food and, as the name suggests, ale. Sometimes an ox or a sheep would be given by a farmer and roasted. There was dancing and games, the celebrations often lasting several days. Joseph Strutt in *Sports and Pastimes of the People of England* recorded:

The Church-ales, called also Easter-ales, and Whitsun-ales from their being sometimes held on Easter-Sunday, and on Whit-Sunday, or on some of the holidays that follow them, certainly originated from the wakes. The churchwardens and other chief parish officers observing

30

the wakes to be more popular than any other holidays, rightly conceived, that by establishing other institutions somewhat similar to them, they might draw together a large company of people, and annually collect from them, gratuitously as it were, such sums of money for the support and repair of the church, as would be a great easement to the parish rates. By some enticement to the populance they brewed a certain portion of strong ale, to be ready on the day appointed for the festival, which they sold to them. . . .

Using the church as a market also seems to have been customary on the Feast Day of St Ulric (4 July)—in this case the commodity was fish. The translation of *Naogeorgus* by Barnaby Googe includes the following verse:

> Wheresoeuer Huldryche hath his place,
>   The people there brings in
> Both Carpes and Pykes and Mullets fat,
>   Has favour here to win.
> Amid the church there sitteth one,
>   And to the Aulter nie,
> That selleth fish, and so good cheep,
>   That every man may buie.

Woolwich—now part of South East London—had two saints' celebrations. The Feast Day of St Catherine of Alexandria (25 November) was commemorated at the Royal Arsenal up to the mid-19th century by a parade round the town, the feature being a man dressed as a woman and rolling a large wheel, representing the wheel upon which the saint was martyred.

Also at the Royal Arsenal in Woolwich, the apprentices marched on the Feast Day of St Clement (23 November), the patron saint of blacksmiths, with a ceremony involving the crowning of 'Old Clem'. This custom was continued until well into the 19th century. Before the Reformation the day was universally marked by processions of children bedecked in flowers.

Another marching celebration took place on St Crispin's Day (25 October) at Newcastle-on-Tyne, when the cordwainers held a coronation of their patron saint by marching in procession from the Freemason's Hospital, Westgate, through Gateshead, and coming to a halt at an inn called the Chancellor's Head, Newgate, to dine. The celebration is believed to have been held regularly until 1789 when it lost its following, to be revived only once in 1822.

The Feast of St John (27 December) is the day of the Freemason's Walk at Melrose, Roxburghshire, which dates from 1707.

Members of the Lodge of Melrose St John march through the town by torchlight to Melrose Abbey.

Processions play a prominent part in Saint's Day festivals. At one time in the history of the Charlton Horn Fair on St Luke's Day (18 October), a procession was formed from the inns of Bishopsgate to march to Charlton. This was headed by a king, queen, miller, councillor and others with horns on their heads. On arrival at Charlton the assembly marched three times round the church.

The Christ's Hospital School March in London takes place on St Matthew's Day (21 September), when three hundred Bluecoat boys from the Horsham School and twenty-five girls from the Hertford School, form up at Sepulchre's Church, Newgate, and march to the Mansion House, where each of the children receive a silver coin from the Lord Mayor of London.

The Congleton, Cheshire, St Peter-ad-Vincula Day (1 August) festivities, up to the time of the Reformation, involved a procession of men wearing heavy leather belts hung with bells, the sound of which was meant to represent St Peter's chains. When the religious motive for the celebration was suppressed after the Reformation, the belts fell into the hands of a family of chimney sweeps who, either through ignorance or profanity, debased the ceremony into a drunken parade, making a parody of religious worship at the Market Cross. In the middle of the 19th century, the people of Congleton, out of patience with such rowdiness, encouraged the Town Clerk to put an end to the celebration. After the usual

Anglo-Saxon Dance

32

Mummers

drunken behaviour and some running fights, the leaders, owners of the belts, were arrested and put in the jail overnight. The following morning they were offered their freedom and a sum of money if they would give up their claim to the belts. This was agreed and the belts went into the custody of the Corporation.

In the Middle Ages, Christians, strongly influenced by pagan customs, used strange symbolisms in their manifestations of worship. For instance, at Aix-in-Provence, France, on Corpus Christi Day (2 June) it was customary to pay homage to the finest tom cat that could be found. The animal was wrapped in swaddling clothes and exhibited at a shrine. Later in the year, at the Feast of St John, the unfortunate cats were put to death by being burned alive in baskets while the clergy conducted a religious ceremony. The reason for this ritual is obscure but the manner of burning alive in baskets is reminiscent of the Druid's form of human sacrifice.

Animals had a rough time on Saints' Days. The Feast of St Luke (18 October) was known as Whip Dog Day. Boys roamed round the streets of towns, whipping all the dogs that were unfortunate enough to be found. The popular explanation is that it originated in the Middle Ages when a priest, while celebrating the Mass, dropped the pix and the consecrated bread was promptly swallowed by a dog.

It seems that not only dogs were whipped on St Luke's Day. Even more bizarre was the whipping of women with furze on Blackheath on the day of the St Luke's Charlton Horn Fair. There was a saying, 'all's fair at the Horn Fair', and there was certainly some boisterous behaviour. Mobs used to meet at Cockold's Point near Deptford, to march from Greenwich to Charlton. The men were dressed as women and many carried horns on their heads.

From early records it is clear that horns were carried or displayed at the Charlton Fair at least as early as 1598. The association with St Luke is thought to have originated from representations of the saint with an ox or a cow by his side.

Bonfires form an important part of the tradition of St John's

Eve (23 June). A chain of fires is still lit along the Cornish hills, the start of which is at St Ives. Only the Cornish language is spoken at this revel and flowers are thrown on the sea.

The word *bonfire* is generally accepted to have been derived from *bone* fire and, strictly, the term should only apply when bones are used. To quote Homily, three types of fire were lit:

Clene bones and noo woode. Bone fore to frighten dragons. Clene woode and no bones, for people to sit and wake thereby. Woode and bones and is called Saynt Johannys Fyre. The first fyre, as the great clerke Johan Belleth telleth, he was in a certayne countrey, so in this countrey there was soo greate hete, the which caused that dragons to go togyther in tekenynge, that Johan dyed in brennyge love and charyte to God and men, and they that dye in charyte shall have part of all good prayers, and they that do not, shall never be saved. Then as these dragons flewe in th'ayre they shed down to that water froth of ther kynde, and so envenyned the waters, and caused soche peopel for to take theyr deth thereby, and many dyverse sykenesse. Wyse clerkes knoweth well that dragons hate nothyng more than the stenche of brennynge bones, and therefore they gadryd as many as they mighte fynde and brent them; and so with the stenche thereof they drove away the dragons, and so they were brought out of greete dysease. The seconde fyre was made of woode, for that wyll brenne lyght, and

34

wyll be see farre. For it is the chefe of fyre to be seen farre, and betoken-
nynge that Saynt Johan was a lanterne of lyght to the people. Also
the people made blazes of fyre for that they shulde be seene farre, and
specyally in the nyght, in token of S. Johan having been seen from
farre in the spirit of Jeremiah. The third fyre of bones betokenneth
Johan's martyrdome, for his bones were brent.

Interesting as this explanation is, the historian Brand referred to
it as 'a pleasant absurdity'.

The Feast Day of St John the Apostle (27 December), not to be
confused with St John the Baptist, was one of the several days in
the church calendar when a Festival of Fools was celebrated,
within as well as outside the churches. People in ridiculous
clothing ate and drank in the church and played dice on the altar
steps while the service was in progress.

A ceremony, obviously related to the various Festivals of Fools,
was the election and investment of the Boy Bishop on St Nicholas
Day (6 December) and on the Feast of the Holy Innocents
(28 December). One of the choir boys was chosen and pro-
claimed bishop for the day. Like many other customs concerning
the church, the investing of the boy bishops came to an end in the
reign of Henry VIII, but was revived to some extent in 1554,
when a boy bishop was featured in a London procession.

Martinmas (11 November) at Fenny Stratford in Buckingham-

Valentine's Day

Fenny Poppers

shire has been celebrated for many years by the ceremony known as the Firing of the Poppers. The *poppers* are metal pots weighing about 20lb each. These are kept in the church belfry and, for the day, are taken out into a nearby field, filled with gunpowder and fired at four-hourly intervals, commencing at 8 o'clock in the morning. The people of Fenny Stratford do not confine their poppers to Martinmas, they are also fired on occasions of national rejoicing. St Martin of Tours was a soldier and possibly this form of celebration of the Feast Day was chosen as it had a warlike effect.

There are mentions of an old Lincolnshire celebration on St Thomas's Day (21 December), which went under the curious name of 'Mumping'. Unfortunately no details of the custom have survived. However, it seems that only women and one member of each family took part. If a woman could not attend, she was permitted to send a child as a deputy. It may or may not have had connections with a Festival of Fools.

Apart from theories of pagan origins and that birds are supposed to mate on this day, according to the *Etymological Dictionary*

Wheel Rolling on
St Catherine's Day

St Giles Fair at Oxford

(Menage), and *Shakespeare and His Times* (Drake), the association between Valentine's Day (14 February) and lovers stems from a Madame Royale, daughter of Henry IV of France, who built a palace in Turin and gave it the name 'Valentine' in honour of the saint. At the first party held there, Madame Royale arranged that lots should be drawn to decide for each lady who should be her lover of the year. The ladies received nosegays from their lovers and the men were given trappings to put on their horses. These parties became known as Valentines.

A Valentine custom used to be practised in the West Country. Three single men went out before daylight in an attempt to catch an owl and two sparrows. If successful, they carried the birds to the inn before the females got up. Here, each of the men were rewarded with a pot of *purl*.* As symbols, the owl represented wisdom and the sparrows lovers.

* Purl is a spiced and warmed ale.

37

Although not specifically related to Valentine's Day, there was a charming Elizabethan custom of a girl giving love tokens to her swain on this day. In the 18th century, these took the form of small handkerchiefs about three inches square with a button or tassel at each corner and embroidered in gold. The men wore the tokens in their hats.

In the early part of the 19th century, the village of Swaffham in Norfolk made much of Valentine's Day, although the celebration here was held on 13 February. Valentine letters were attached to apples and oranges, front doors slyly opened, the gifts thrown in and the anonymous donor was heard running up the street. Some jokers would show their sense of fun by chalking white squares on doorsteps to make those who lived within think that a letter had been delivered.

4. Seasonal Festivals

The annual seasonal festivals that have survived through the centuries have, without exception, their roots and traditions in ancient pagan celebrations. Often these were adopted by the Christian Church and modified to embrace various facets of the faith.

The best example of Christian adoption is that of Christmas itself. The ancient Egyptians celebrated the Nativity of the Sun in midwinter, as did the Persians in their Mithraic religion. The Romans, from early times, held their Festival of Saturnalia about this time of the year, with evergreens as symbolic decorations. Presents were exchanged and it was customary for the roles of master and slave to be reversed. On the several occasions when attempts have been made to suppress the celebration of Christmas, it has been these pagan origins that have been cited as the reason. The early Christians did not approve of present giving at Christmas because of the connection with Saturnalia, and Cromwell put a stop to the festival in its entirety, as did Lenin—but for different reasons.

When the Romans settled in Britain they probably brought the present-giving custom with them. In time it became accepted practice to exchange gifts of gloves, first at New Year and then at Christmas. 'Thrift Boxes' were placed in shops and customers were invited to make donations for the apprentices.

Most forms of Christmas celebrations we have today are of 19th century origin, although it must not be assumed that our more distant ancestors ignored the festival. It has always been a time for feasting and dancing, for plays and games, and for decorating the home and church with evergreens for the twelve day duration.

There is a surviving custom at Bridgnorth, Salop, which seems to have its roots in earlier times. On Boxing Day youths perform mock singlestick battles in the town and collect money from passers by. In other places it was the custom to play the barbaric form of mass-football that was prevalent before the game was regulated in the mid-19th century.

At Brough, Westmorland (now Cumbria), up to the middle of the 19th century, a holly tree was carried in procession on

The Boar's Head at Christmas

39

Twelfth Night. In the latter years of the ceremony's enactment, an ash tree was substituted as this species was more common than holly in the district. To each branch was fastened a lighted torch. Starting at 8 o'clock in the evening, the tree was carried up and down the streets after which it was erected at the town centre to be danced round. The two inns each year alternately provided the refreshment.

The New Year celebration of Hogmany (Hogmenay), almost certainly has its origin in an ancient Celtic pagan rite of mid-winter, called *hoggin-nott* or *hogenat*, meaning a slaughter night. After the common acceptance of Christianity the celebration was kept up in places, notably in Scotland.

In the 18th century the young men of northern towns and villages, wearing masks, crooked horns, false beards, ancient coats and paper caps, visited shops and houses, demanding their hogmany money or refreshment. In country districts they called at farmhouses and, unless told the 'old style' was kept—whatever that might mean—would perform a hogmany drama, the details of which have been lost through time, although it was probably based on the story of the Roman occupation under Agricola.

New Year has considerable connections with fire. One surviving celebration is the Homany Flambeaux at Comrie, Perthshire, in which people carry firebrands in procession led by a piper to the town square for merrymaking.

At Allendale, Northumberland, there is a similar revel at New Year. In the procession, men in fancy dress carry forty tubs of burning pitch to be thrown on the town's bonfire. Even during the blackout days of World War II, the revel was continued with the fires carried in covered biscuit tins.

When the New Year bells are rung at Stonehaven, Kincardineshire, the Swinging of the Fireballs begins. The balls are made from wire netting and filled with oil-soaked rags and swung around the heads of men marching in procession.

Of all the January fire revels, that of Up Helly Aa, held at Lerwick in the Shetland Islands on the last Tuesday in the month, must be the most spectacular. A *guiser jarl*—master of ceremonies—is appointed and his word is law for the day. For several weeks work has been in progress on the building of a 30ft replica of a Viking ship. In the evening a procession is formed,

Carrying the Hollytree at Brough

41

Twelfth Night

the ship leading a number of squads of men, each squad in distinctive uniform and carrying flaming torches. At Clickimen Loch they sing the traditional *Norseman's Home* and set fire to the ship. It is said to commemorate the coming of the sun in the winter months and to have originated during the Norse occupation of the islands and the consequent suppression of Christianity.

The word *shrove* is derived from the fact that people were *shriven* or absolved from sin after confession. Up to the time of the Reformation there were four recognised days of Shrovetide: Shrove Saturday, Shrove Sunday, Callop or Shrove Monday, and Shrove Tuesday. Only the latter remains to mark the prelude to the six weeks of Lent with its associated fasting.

Apart from religious ceremonies and customs, it was the

practice in country districts for the youths to run round the villages carrying firebrands and torches.

Pancakes became traditional fare as they were a convenient way of using the surplus eggs and fats that would not be needed during the period of Lent. It has been said that the Druids cooked pancakes over mistletoe fires at this time of the year—the mistletoe being left over from the mid-winter celebrations—but this may be romantic speculation.

Shrovetide was one of the traditional times when mass-football games were played with entire male populations of the villages taking part, often resulting in injuries and sometimes even deaths.

A Shrovetide custom that fortunately died out about the middle of the nineteenth century was the practice of Shying at Tethered Cocks. In some parts of the country the cock was suspended in an earthenware pot over the street, the person succeeding in breaking the pot being the winner of the cock.

Threshing the Hen was another barbaric Shrove custom in which the hen was battered to death, cooked and eaten. Tusser, in a book, *Five Hundred Points of Good Husbandry* (1620), described how the hen was hung on the back of a man who had horsebells suspended around his neck. Other men, blindfolded, attempted to follow the man by the sound of the bells and beat the hen to death with clubs.

Cocks and hens have featured in Shrovetide customs from very early times. According to Fitzstephen, writing in the reign of Henry II, on the morning of Shrove Tuesday 'the school boys of the City of London bring game cocks to their masters, and in the fore part of the day, till dinner time, they are permitted to amuse themselves with seeing them fight'.

The idea of the fasting period of Lent was not universally welcomed. There was an early 19th century custom on Ash

Hen Threshing
Right: Shying at Cocks

Wednesday for people to parade through the streets with herrings nailed to poles. The procession was accompanied by chanting:

> Herrings, herrings, stinking herrings.
> No more puddings.

The participants then indulged in ducking one another in the village pond—the idea of this being to wash away the effects of the feasting in preparation for Lent.

In other places young girls were harnessed to ploughs and driven along the streets. The reason for this custom and its origin is obscure. This may also be said of the strange practice of tossing dogs in the air at Shrovetide.

Another example of a pagan festival adopted by the Christian Church is Mothering Sunday in mid-Lent. It has its origin in the Roman celebration of Hilaria in praise of the 'mother of the gods'. The pagan element survived for many centuries in a custom involving youths parading with a figure of death—probably depicting the end of winter. The ceremony took an alternative form in some places with figures representing Spring and Winter. Boys fought in mock battles in which Spring was the victor.

The mid-Lent Sunday later became the traditional day on which gifts and cakes were presented to mothers. At Bristol, in the 18th century, special 'Mothering Cakes' were made, decorated by local artists.

Mid-Lent Sunday
Winter and Spring

Eggs have been associated with Spring celebrations since long before Christians commemorated Christ's crucifixion and the rising from the tomb. Eggs were adopted as being symbolic of the stone that was rolled away from the tomb. Pace, Paste or Pask eggs—the words derived from *pasch*, the Jewish passover— were at one time consecrated before being used in ritualistic games. There are many egg rolling and egg tapping ceremonies in widespread areas, a great proportion of which survive as children's games. Avenham Park, Preston, where brightly coloured hard-boiled eggs are rolled down hill on Easter Monday, at Scarborough, and at West Derby near Liverpool, to mention only three places where the practice is continued. The men of West Derby, in the last century, would meet on Easter Sunday in patched inside-out clothing, visiting the houses to beg for eggs, oatmeal cakes and money, after which they proceeded to the alehouse to indulge in merrymaking.

A strange Easter celebration is to be found in The Bottle Kicking and Hare Pie Scrambling at Hallerton in Leicestershire, which is still performed on Easter Monday. Two hare pies are blessed by the vicar after which slices of the pies are thrown into the assembled crowd at a place known as Hare Pie Bank. The *bottles* are three casks, two of which are filled with beer. The empty cask is thrown three times into the air by the 'Custodian of the

Maypole in the Strand

Bottle', thus starting the game between villagers of Hallerton and Medbourne, the object of which is to score a goal by getting a bottle across one of two stones, a mile apart.

A ceremony, said to date from the time of Edward I and still being enacted at the beginning of the 19th century was that of Lifting and Heaving. It is known that the custom used to take place at Easter in Shropshire, Staffordshire, Warwickshire and Lancashire, and probably in other counties. Men lifted women and vice versa in the street. At the Talbot Inn, Shrewsbury, the serving girls would lift visitors for a small fee. The origin of this custom is unknown but perhaps one may speculate that there is a connection with the 'chairing' of the Pope.

One had to be careful in the North of England towns at Eastertide during the 18th and 19th centuries. In Durham at 4 o'clock in the afternoon of Easter Sunday, groups of lads would wander about the streets accosting females and forcibly removing their shoes. 'Pay for your shoes, if you please', was the demand

and a penny had to be paid before they were returned. On the following day, Easter Monday, it was the girls' turn to play the trick on the males. If boots with difficult-to-untie laces were worn, it was the hat that was taken. By 1826 the ransom had increased to six pence.

The festivities on May Day have their roots in Floralia, the Roman feast to Flora, the goddess of Spring and flowers, said to have been a celebrated courtesan who bequeathed a fortune to the people of Rome so they would annually make merry in her name. The festival began with the sound of a trumpet, whereupon courtesans were called upon to dance naked in the streets.

May Day continued to be observed in Christian times but the saints' days had the prominent place as excuses for public celebrations. After the Reformation and the abandonment of the Catholic saints' days, May Day took on greater significance. It became the great rural festival, with every door and window adorned in May blossom before dawn.

Henry VIII was a May Day enthusiast. One year, while riding with his court on a Maying from Greenwich to the high ground on Shooter's Hill, he was met by two hundred archers

May Day at Hitchin

led by 'Robin Hood', who ordered them to let off their arrows in one flight, much to the delight of the king. 'Robin Hood' is the English 'Lord of the May'—in some places known as 'Jack-o'-the-Green'—whose task at the celebrations was to dance around with a long stick adorned with a floral wreath.

Not every May Day celebration occurs on 1 May. At Ickwell, Bedfordshire, for instance, the May Day Revel is, to this day, performed on 25 May. The attendants of the Ickwell May Queen are two characters known as 'Moggies' who carry collecting boxes and brooms, for some obscure reason.

The early 19th century was a golden age for individual-style May Day celebrations prior to the Victorian movement towards standardisation when the May revelling comprised mainly the crowning of the May Queen and dancing around the Maypole. At Penzance the celebration began on May Eve, the young men and girls starting a midnight parade complete with a small band, calling at farmhouses where they were presented with 'heavy country cake' and tea, rum and milk. In return for this hospitality they performed a dance which went on through the night. Part of the celebration consisted of the making of 'May Music'. To perform this, a circle was cut in the bark of a may branch, the bark was tapped away and a hole cut through which it was possible to blow.

Hitchin in Hertfordshire had a singular custom. In this the Mayers paraded through the town at 3 o'clock in the morning,

Jack-o'-the-Green

singing a May Song and carrying large bunches of may, attaching sprigs to door knockers as they passed. At the houses of unpopular members of the community bunches of elder tree and nettles were fixed. This was an all-male parade, but some were dressed as women. There was 'Mad Moll' and her husband—the male partner with his face blackened and a hump on his back and carrying a birch broom. Another 'couple' were finely dressed and called the 'Lord and Lady'.

A reminder of the pagan origin of May Day celebrations was to be found in a custom, at Holme, Devon, in which a lamb was caught and slaughtered on a granite slab by the cutting of its throat, after which the beast was roasted whole and the pieces of meat scrambled for.

The name of the West London area of Mayfair commemorates the annual great fair which was held until about 1766, around the village of Shepherd's Market. South of the market was a noted ducking pond on which competitions were held. Dogs were let loose and the first to bring out a duck was declared the winner. The activity was a popular gambling pastime in the reign of Charles II. For the period of the fair a theatre was improvised on the first floor of the Market House, and a montebanks' stage erected near the Three Jolly Butchers public house at the eastern end of the market. Mingling with the crowds were toymen and gingerbread bakers. Sideshows included booths for jugglers, prize fighters, cudgel play and the back sword, boxing matches,

Northampton May
Garland

wild beasts, fire eaters, sausage tables, Ups and Downs (the big wheel), hand-driven Merry Go Rounds, strong woman acts, and a gruesome puppet show representing the execution of Lord Lovat. For the more competitive minded merrymakers there was ass-racing, bull-baiting, grinning for a hat, running for a shift, hasty pudding eating and eel diving.

An ancient Irish May Day celebration, carried on until well into the 19th century, was *la ne beal tina* dedicated to the god Beal. On the evening and night before the day the 'good people' were supposed to possess an inclination towards all manner of mischief, while youths and girls were considered susceptible to all kinds of evil. A reminder of the worship of Beal is to be found in the ritual of making cows jump over a straw fire in order to save the milk being pilfered by the 'good people'. On May Day itself, the girls danced and the youths engaged in hurling and other athletic pursuits. They marched through the streets in three divisions, with young men in the van and at the rear. Two of the girls carried a holly bush each, on which were hung hurling balls, the girls' presents to the boys. Music was provided by bagpipes or military fife, drum and tamboreen. Accompanying the parade was a clown carrying a mop which he dipped in puddles and sprinkled the crowd. Somewhat more irritatingly, a few youths rushed about, hitting out at the onlookers with bunches of stinging nettles.

May Day at Lynn

It was customary to make fools, or 'May Goslings', of people on May Day by methods similar to those used on April the first. If there was an attempt to make a May Gosling on 2 May, it was usual to reply:

> May Day's past and gone.
> Thou's a gosling, and I'm none.

The maypole has obscure origins. We know that in the 15th century it was the custom for the owners of estates to erect a pole around which the servants of the house could enact a May Day play. The standard form of this play featured the 'Lord of the May' in the character of Robin Hood, attended by Friar Tuck and Maid Marion.

Maypoles were an essential part of the London scene. In Leadenhall Street, for instance, a maypole stood outside the church of St Andrew. In 1517, the London apprentices rioted against foreign merchants and in an attempt to reduce the inflammatory mood, the maypole was taken down. Thereafter it lay flat by the church door until being sawn up and burned in 1552.

Like everything else connected with pleasure, the maypole was banned under the Commonwealth and was not permitted again until after the Restoration in 1661. The new freedom was celebrated in the Strand by the erection of a 134ft pole at the

Country Maypole

junction of Catherine Street. At the end of Little Drury Lane, a smith, by the name of George Clarges, erected a maypole to commemorate his daughter's marriage to General Monck, who was to become the first Duke of Albermarle. Other famous maypoles in London that survived until about 1795 included one at Kennington Green, at the corner of Workhouse Lane leading from Vauxhall Road to Elizabeth Place, near the Black Horse public house.

A May month festival of ancient origin was observed in Scotland up to the 18th century in honour of Beal, the sun god. This took several forms. For instance, in the parish of Callendar on *Beltein Day*, a trench was cut round the assembled crowd. A fire was built in the middle of the area on which was cooked a custard of eggs and milk. An oatmeal cake was also cooked and divided into as many portions as there were people. One portion was blackened with charcoal and put with the others into a bonnet. These were drawn and the person with the black piece was 'devoted to be sacrificed to Beal'. This was not as unpleasant as it sounds, it being necessary to jump through the fire three times.

Whitsuntide is the Feast of Pentecost. Originally a Jewish festival, observed fifty days after the offering of the wave-sheaf on the second day of unleavened bread—the festival known as Passover. When the feast was included in the Christian Church calendar it became commemorative of the descent of the Holy Spirit. *Whit* is supposed to be derived from the wearing of white garments by those prepared for baptism on this day.

At the Whit Monday Ram Fair at Kingsteignton, Devon, the carcass of a ram is carried in procession through the streets before being roasted whole over an open fire. The fair is said to commemorate a time when a ram was sacrificed in the hope that the gods would cause a water spring to erupt.

Whitsuntide, in the reign of Richard I, was time for horse

Milkmaids' Dance

racing along the bank of the river Fleet in London in order to prove worth before being sold at Smithfield.

Generally, at the opening of the 19th century, when fairs had lost their importance as markets, they had become bawdy and disreputable affairs. There were exceptions. At Necton, Norfolk, in 1817, for example, a Major Mason staged the first annual Whitsuntide Fair as a more genteel festival of rural sports. Later the event was known as the Necton Guild. The usual rural attractions were staged: wrestling, foot-races, jingling matches, jumping in sacks, blindfolded wheelbarrow races, spinning matches, whistling matches, grinning through the horsecollar, and leaping matches. The Necton Guild also featured a maypole, a mask and morris dancing.

There is a Cornish midsummer ceremony that is reputed to owe its origins to the Druids. This was the carrying of firebrands round the streets, known as the Sacrifice to Apollo. Similar celebrations were carried out in Ireland, the sacrifices there being directed to Baal, Beal or Bealin—the god of the sun. Brand mentions this Beal tradition in an article in the *Gentleman's Magazine* in 1795, fixing the chief festival of the sun in Ireland as 21 June. On this date cattle were led round the fire, while those attending the fire leapt through the flames.

Planting the Village Maypole

In pagan times, at the time of harvest, sacrifices were made to the goddess Vacuna (Vacina). As was the case with many pagan customs, the Christian Church was quick to realise the benefit in carrying on the traditions, transforming the rituals into Harvest Thanksgiving Festivals.

The more interesting celebrations took place, not in the churches, but in the harvest fields themselves. There was a begging custom in Suffolk in which a *mylord* was chosen from among the harvest workers. When a traveller was seen approaching, the mylord's task was to go up to the stranger and ask him for a *largess* (*sic*)—a sum of money. If successful he would mount a tree stump and recite a couplet with all the harvesters standing in a circle. They then placed their sickles within the circle and let out three hearty cheers. The money so collected was, of course, spent on ale in the evening. In Suffolk the custom was known as Begging a Largess, in Norfolk as Largess Hallo'ed. In both counties the result was a 'going for a whet' to the alehouse.

Up to about 1780 at Bridlington and other parts of Yorkshire there was held a ceremony that went under the name of Burning the Witch. It was a feast in the harvest field in the evening after the last of the corn had been cut. Ale and burnt pies were the main ingredients of the feast.

At Hitchin in Hertfordshire, the Harvest Home celebration involved the farmer driving the last load like fury while the workers ran after the wagon with bowls of water, trying to soak the corn.

Most Hallowe'en customs seem to have the purpose of countering the influences of witches and demons, or to foretell the future. Many, it is thought, owe their origins to Druidism and pagan festivals, and have persisted despite the Christian Church's efforts to ban them. In the so-called witches' covens, Hallowe'en is taken very seriously. The High Priestesses celebrate with special rites to conjure up the souls of the dead loved ones and prayers are offered to the 'god of the witches'. After dancing in the nude, fires are lit on the *altar* and at the four compass points.

Hallowe'en owes what religious significance it has to Pope Gregory III (731–41), who assigned 31 October for celebrating the consecration of a chapel in St Paul's Basilica to all the saints.

Hallowe'en is known by various names, depending on the part of the country. At Hinton St George, Somerset, it is called Punkey Night (*punkies* being the lanterns made from mangel-

Harvest Home at
Hawkesbury,
Cotswolds

wurzels), at Newcastle-on-Tyne it is known as Dookie Apple Night, and at Swansea it is called Apple and Candle Night.

The night has long been an excuse for indoor merrymaking which has featured such delights as Bob Apple, Strung Apples, or Dookie Apples, with apples either suspended on string or floating in a bowl of water. Some historians suggest these games with apples have their roots in ancient pagan rites. In the Isle of Lewis at Hallowe'en a sacrifice was made to the sea god Shony, until the early part of the 19th century. The villagers gathered at the church of St Mulvey after brewing ale from home-grown malt. A chosen man then carried a cup of the ale into the sea, saying, 'Shony, I give you this cup of ale, hoping you will be so kind as to send us pleanty of sea ware, and enriching our ground thro' the ensuing year'. He then threw the cup of ale into the sea, rejoined his companions and then they all began the business of seeing to it that no more of the ale was wasted.

5. Commemorative Celebrations and Proclaiming Rights

Commemorating events of national and even minor importance has long been a preoccupation of civilised society. Military victories and even defeats are commemorated usually only in the lifespan of the survivors. Trafalgar Day no longer has any significance and even the importance of 11 November, the anniversary of the end of World War I—an event still within the memory of many—has diminished almost to obscurity. However, most historical events continue to be remembered somewhere.

The excuse for the people of Newark to make merry on 30 January each year up to the early 1800s was the commemoration of the execution of Charles I. This was called Oranges and Bells Day. The market stallholders stocked only oranges which were raffled by means of a 24-sided dice, about the size of a hen's egg, being rolled down a pipe. Church bells rang from six in the morning until eight in the evening and gambling went on in the taverns all through the night.

Customs like this at Newark, celebrating the execution of Charles I had a Commonwealth bias, but the other side have been represented and one that still continues to this day is the dressing with flowers of the king's statue in Whitehall, London.

The most famous of surviving Restoration commemorations is the Founder's Day at the Royal Hospital, Chelsea, on 29 May each year when Charles II statute is decorated with sprigs of oak—to mark the king's escape in the Boscobel Oak. After a march and inspection parade the pensioners of the hospital celebrate with plum pudding and beer.

On 29 May each year at Scotland Street, Sheffield, was held the Scotland Feast in commemoration of the Restoration of the monarchy. Up to the early part of the 19th century it was customary to set up twenty trees each year, symbolic of the oak that harboured Charles II. Appropriately, there was a public house in the street called The Royal Oak which, of course, acted as the headquarters for the celebration. The activities comprised ass races, foot races, grinning matches and shows by montebanks and merryandrews.

Still in Yorkshire on 29 May, this time in Richmond, the

Above: Mischief Night at Leeds
Right: Bonfire Night at Lewes

Restoration was celebrated by a procession and a performance of the Robin Hood play that lasted for two days.

Restoration commemorations were not confined to the North of England. Tiverton, Devon had its own very important festivity with a procession of young men dressed in 17th century costume and carrying swords. Four of the men carried a throne with a child seated upon it. A character depicting Oliver Cromwell, his hands and face smeared with black grease, was led by means of a cord around his body by others in the procession. Oliver's trick was to leap out and attempt to smear the onlookers with grease.

The Gunpowder Plot is mainly celebrated on 5 November but, in some places on the nearest Saturday. Effigies of Guy Fawkes are burned at Lewes, Sussex, where there are six bonfire societies. In the castle grounds there is an iron vehicle with wheels, on which tar barrels were rolled through the streets to the huge bonfire escorted by a torchlight procession.

Guy Fawkes was born at York in a house which is now the Young's Hotel, in the shadow of the Minster. Here in York the commemoration of 5 November is called Mischief Night.

The Marks for Allotting Dolemoors

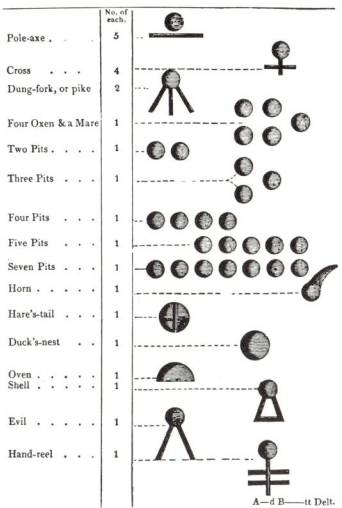

	No. of each.	
Pole-axe .	5	
Cross . . .	4	
Dung-fork, or pike	2	
Four Oxen & a Mare	1	
Two Pits	1	
Three Pits . . .	1	
Four Pits . . .	1	
Five Pits . . .	1	
Seven Pits . . .	1	
Horn	1	
Hare's-tail	1	
Duck's-nest . .	1	
Oven	1	
Shell : : : : :	1	
Evil	1	
Hand-reel . . .	1	

A—d B——tt Delt.

The Doctor Johnson commemoration is held at Lichfield, Staffordshire, his birthplace, each year on the Saturday nearest 18 September. It involves a mayoral procession to Dr Johnson's statue in the market square where a laurel wreath is laid, and Johnson's prayer is read at the house of his birth. There follows a supper of steak, kidney and mushroom pudding, apple tart and cream, ale and hot punch—the good doctor's favourite meal.

Riding the Black Lad was a symbolically barbaric celebration performed until the early years of the 19th century at Ashton-under-Lyme. On Easter Monday a figure of a man was made up from an old suit and carried through the streets of the town on a horse. During the ride the effigy was shot at by anyone who happened to have a gun at the ready. The figure was then taken off the horse, tied against a post and shot at continuously until set on fire, after which it was torn to pieces.

The origin of the ceremony is obscure. It has been suggested that it was a mark of disrespect for a landowning family or perhaps it marked the killing of some tyrant. It has further been suggested that it may have something to do with the knighthood bestowed on Thomas Ashton by Edward III, an unpopular granting of the accolade.

The unexpected appearance of a prince in some bygone age at Restormel Castle, near Lostwithiel, Cornwall, is thought to have been the origin of an Easter Sunday celebration that used to take place until late in the 19th century.

Bonfire Night at Ottery St Mary

Penny for the Guy

The freeholders of Lostwithiel each year elected one of their number to act as the 'prince'. Richly attired, mounted on a white horse, with crown on the head and sceptre in hand, he was met at the church gate by the minister. After the service there was a reception where the 'prince' was entertained as royalty.

The origin of the Fairlop Fair in Hainault Forest, Essex, has been attributed to one, Daniel Day, a Wapping blockmaker who had come to live nearby in the early 19th century. Being a man of sociable disposition, he gave a dinner each year on the last Friday in July, feeding bacon and beans to all comers. By 1725 a popular amusement and marketing fair had been established. It became the custom for Wapping blockmakers to bring a longboat mounted on a carriage, gaily decorated for the merrymaking. The Fairlop Fair was discontinued in 1853.

In 1782, John Knell of St Ives, Cornwall, bequeathed the income from his estate to provide prizes for racing, rowing and wrestling, to be held every fifth year 'for ever'. The first gathering was held in 1801 and an eyewitness at the time recorded:

Early in the morning the roads from Helston, Truro and Penzance were lined with horses and vehicles of every description, while thousands of travellers on foot poured in from all quarters till noon, when the assembly formed. The wrestlers entered the ring; the troop of virgins, dressed in white, advanced with solemn step to the notes of harmony; the spectators ranged themselves along the hills; at length the mayor of St Ives appeared in his robes of state. The signal was given; the flags were displayed in waving splendour from the towers of the castle; the sight was grand. Here the wrestlers exerted their sinewy strength; there the rowers in their various dresses of blue, white and red, urged the gilded prows of their boats through the sparkling waves—the dashing of the oars—the songs of the virgins— all joined to enliven the picture. The ladies and gentlemen of Penzance returned to an elegant dinner at the Unicorn Hotel and a splendid ball concluded the evening entertainments.

Although, in general, doles and charities do not come within the scope of this book, it is felt that one example should be mentioned.

The village of Avening in Gloucestershire possesses a church consecrated in the year 1080. It is reputed that on the day a feast was given by Queen Matilda. Since then, on the Sunday following 14 September, has been held what is known locally as Pig-Face Day, at which pig-face sandwiches are served after the sermon.

Whitsuntide is the traditional time when the boundaries of the parish are either walked over, ridden over, boys beaten or bumped, or simply the boundary posts thrashed.

The first Thursday in June is the day on which the Lanark boundaries are inspected and wreaths laid on the Wallace statute. Through the decorated town there is a procession called the Birks—because birch branches are carried. Later in the day another procession, led by the 'Lord Cornet', starts off from the town to ride the marshes. In this latter celebration a silver bell, said to date from about 1100, is rung.

Hocktide is the ancient Saxon time for determining boundaries and proclaiming rights—since the establishment of the Christian calendar it marks the Monday and Tuesday after the second Sunday following Easter. At Hungerford, Berkshire, at the time

Sword Dance

Beating the Bounds at
the Tower of London

of John o'Gaunt, the Hocktide Revel was founded. The tradition
is that John o'Gaunt gave the Hungerford people free use of the
common land and granted fishing rights in river Kennet. The
celebration survives today when the Hungerford Hocktide Tutti-
Men perform. On the Tuesday, dressed in top hats and tailed
coats, carrying long poles adorned with ribbons, spring flowers
and oranges, the Tutti-men parade round the houses of the town,
demanding coins from the men and kisses from the women, in
return for which an orange is given by an accompanying character
called the Orange Scrambler. At the close of the proceedings
the cash and whatever oranges remain are thrown to the children.
Various revels go on through the day, which begins with the
Town Crier blowing on a 17th century horn.

In the parishes of Congresbury and Puxton there are two large
commons known as the East and West Dolemoors (the word
derived from the Saxon *dal* meaning a share or partition). These
commons were divided into equal parts, each with a different

mark cut in the turf, such as a horn, four oxen, a mare, poleaxe, cross, dung fork, oven, duck's nest, hand reel or horse's tail. On the Saturday before Old Midsummer (4 July), the landlords and tenants of Congresbury, Puxton and Week St Lawrence used to meet on the common where they marked apples with the emblems cut in the turf. The apples were put in a sack and picked out at random by the commoners to decide who should have the right to each piece of common land.

At Warkworth, Northamptonshire, the Ashe Meadow was divided into fifteen portions—eight mowers being allocated to each lot. These lots were laid out by six men: two each from Warkworth, Overthorp and Grimsbury, plus one from Nethercote. Two officials called the 'Crocus-Men' and separately known as the 'Bay-Ward' and the 'Master of the Forest', carried the feast on to the field. Traditionally this feast comprised a rump of beef, six penny loaves and three gallons of ale.

65

A woodcutting right is still celebrated at St Briavels, Gloucestershire, a village in the Forest of Dean. The story goes that in the year 1206, the Lord of the Manor granted grazing and woodcutting rights to the villagers on condition that a certain local woman should ride naked down the village street—the challenge was accepted. In recent times the legend has been modified and claims that the right was granted by King John; it is now celebrated by a man standing on the churchyard wall and throwing cubes of bread and cheese to the villagers after a church service.

One of the colourful customs that accompanied proclamations of rights used to take place at Hutton Conyers, near Ripon, on Old New Year's Day (12 January), when the bailiff, the steward and six shepherds from the neighbouring parishes of Melmerby, Bolderby, Newick, Righton and Dishthorp met to arrange the rights of estray on Hutton Moor. Each shepherd brought a large apple pie—the pie from Righton having a double crust and filled with prunes—a two-penny sweetcake and a wooden spoon, except the shepherd from Newick, who gave 16 pence for ale. The bailiff provided furmety,* mustard, cheese and a penny roll. The furmety was put in a pot and buried near the bailiff's house, and the food and ale divided among all present, who drank the health of the Lord of the Manor. If a shepherd forgot to bring a wooden spoon, he would be forced to lay on his face and devour his pie the best way he could while the others gave him a push on the back of the head.

Hot pennies thrown to the children of the town featured in a number of places at the time of the election of a new mayor. Rye in Sussex and Honiton in Devon were two such towns where the custom was performed.

Throwing things seems to be part of several election celebrations. In the 19th century at Kidderminster, on the election of a new bailiff, the inhabitants, on a signal from the Town Hall, threw cabbage stalks at each other for a 'lawless hour', the new bailiff being the main target. It is difficult to suggest an origin for this practice but possibly it was commemorative and symbolic of a public servant being thrown to the populace.

* Furmety, or Frumenty, as it was sometimes called, is a food made from husked wheat boiled in milk.

6. *What Goings On!*

Fool's Baubel

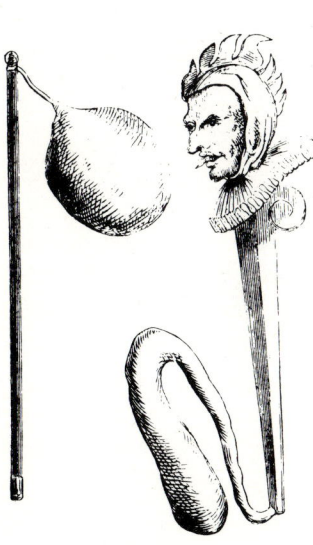

Gentility, mutual respect and kindness to animals had little or no place in the boisterous merrymakings of the past. Hardship of everyday life showed itself in the form of the diverse amusements of the revel. Folk made fools of themselves and others without a second thought, or subjected animals to disgusting degradation and suffering in the cause of pleasure. Typical of such inhumanity were the Bull Runs.

At Stamford each year on 13 November, or—presumably for religious reasons—the nearest weekday when the 13th fell on a Sunday, a Bull Run was held in the town. The excuse for the practice was that it was said to improve the quality of the beef!

The butchers of the town produced a wild bull some days before the Run. Windows were boarded up and guards stationed at the entrances of the town to deter strangers from entering. The bull was released and the population, led by the gaudily dressed 'Bull Queen' (at one time a man dressed as a woman), gave chase, flaying away at the beast with heavy clubs and attempting to corner it on the town bridge, from where it often took a leap into the river. Eventually it was slaughtered and the meat sold. The great gut, or pudding, known as the Tom Hodge, being presented to the best hunter of the day.

The Bull Run is said to have originated in the reign of King John and to have been instigated by William, Earl of Warrenne, who is reputed to have been watching some butchers trying to separate two fighting bulls, when one of the animals ran amok. The good earl gave chase and killed the bull and, feeling that here was good sport, made a bequest of some land to the town on condition the butchers provided a bull each year to be chased by the townsfolk.

Another version of the story is that both the bulls ran down the street chased by dogs and bowling over the population. The earl was apparently doubled up with laughter and wanted to see it all over again. So he made the bequest and specified that the Bull Run be made each year a week before Christmas.

Bull Runs were not only held at Stamford. Tutbury, Staffordshire, was the scene of another event of this type, as part of the August Minstrels Festival. Blount in *The Tenures of Land and*

The Stamford Bull Run

Badger Baiting

Customs of Manors, states that the bull was provided by the bailiff of the manor. The tips of his horns, ears and tail were cut off, his body smeared with soap and his nose blown full of pepper. He was released and the minstrels ran after him trying to cut off a piece of the beast's skin before he crossed the border into Derbyshire. The man who was successful was declared King of the Music's Bull, the bull itself being returned to the High Street to be baited by dogs. If the bull reached Derbyshire without a cut he became the property of the Lord Prior. That, according to Blount, was the original form of the Tutbury Bull Run but later it took another form in which the young men of Staffordshire and of Derbyshire armed themselves with staves and cudgels, and attempted to drive the bull into their respective counties.

The Tutbury Bull Run was outlawed in 1776, by order of the Duke of Devonshire, but it continued illegally until 1840 (the year after the last Stamford Bull Run), when it took Lord John Russell, the then Home Secretary, a regiment of Dragoons and a large force of special constables to stop it.

It is impossible to disassociate cruelty from revels of the past. No fair was without its animal baiting, cock fighting or shying sticks and stones at tethered hens, until these practices were banned by law by the Victorians, and driven underground.

68

Ben White with Dogs

Catching a Soaped or Greased Pig was a feature of country revels until comparatively recent years, and the author can remember, as a boy in the 1930s, seeing pigs being chased at Kentish village fêtes.

A singular form of this animal catching sport used to be enacted on the Monday after Whit Week at Kidlington, Oxfordshire. Only girls of the village took part in the ritual that went under the name of Lady of the Lamb. The competitors had their thumbs tied behind their backs and the girl who caught and held the lamb with her teeth gained the title of Lady of the Lamb, and had the privilege of presiding at a feast held on the following day.

Some of the competitive events at English country fairs and revels in the 17th, 18th and 19th centuries could be observed at all the gatherings. Backswording and singlestick fighting was an expected feature. At the Purton Fair in Wiltshire until 1824, there was an annual match between four men from Purton and four from nearby Stretten. Payment of the expenses for the day fell to the losing side, including a fee for the umpshire (umpire).

Every fair worthy of the name would include Girls Running for Smocks, Climbing the Greasy Pole for a Piece of Bacon, Old Women Drinking Hot Tea for Snuff, Grinning Through the

Horsecollar, Racing Between Old Women for a Pound of Tea, and Leaping in Sacks for a Cheese.

Often merrymaking was nothing more than a few people getting together and having a good time at the expense of others. Typical of this class of revel was the Michaelmas Day Ganging at Bishop's Stortford, which survived well into the 19th century. The youths of the town elected themselves a leader whose role was to take them on a kind of route march. Wherever the leader went the others had to follow—along the streets, through the houses and even wading through ponds and ditches. Anyone unfortunate enough to be in the path of the march was grasped

70

Cock Fighting—detail
from Hogarth

by the arms and bumped against all the members of the gang.
The route was, needless to say, planned to take in many of the
town's taverns and ale houses, the landlords, by tradition, having
to supply a large plum cake and liquid refreshment to the gang.

At the Sherborne Pack Monday Fair in Dorset, youths marched
through the streets at midnight, making as much noise as possible,
as the 'Teddy Roe's Band'. The original character of this name
is said to have been a 15th century mason who led the rest of the
church builders in their celebrating on the first Pack Monday—
the day the workers *packed up* their tools after completing the
work of building the church.

71

Above: Bob Apple
Right: Hoodman Blind

A Remarkable Dance

Feasting and drinking, often immoderately, have always been ingredients of community merrymaking. We find the feast in many religious celebrations, such as Christmas and the Saints' Days. When the Church is not directly involved, it is frequently there in the background.

A man standing outside a church on a Saturday evening in Eastbourne in the early 17th century, carrying a white wand and proclaiming that sops and ale would be given the following day, would not have been a church official but a steward appointed by the married men of the congregation. The 'feast' was to celebrate the birth of a child, and it would seem that women had nothing to do with the event as the sops and ale was strictly a men only affair. The celebration took place in the street after the church service, where three tables were laid out. The first, covered with a white damask cloth, bore a china bowl containing biscuits soaked in wine and fine sugar. At this table sat the men whose wives had borne them twins. The second table's bowl had beer sops and sugar, and the third had a wooden bowl with beer sops and coarse sugar. The last table did not carry the refinement of a table cloth. If a man had any children he sat at the second table but the childless ones had to be content with the third. Toasts were drunk to the new baby and the merrymaking that followed went on well into the night. Views of the ladies about sops and ale are not recorded.

No connection with the Church can be found in the Hitchingstone Feast, which took place on 1 August each year at the place where met the boundaries of Sutton, Cowling, Laycock, Kildwich and Keighley in Yorkshire. The spot was marked by a stone known as the *hitchingstone*. The feast, with its attendant sports and amusements, was typical of simple country revels and would not be worthy of inclusion here if it were not needed as an excuse for relating a little story which reflects the isolation of village communities, difficult to imagine now. The inhabitants of Cowling, or Cowlinghead, were known as 'moons' for the legend goes that a shepherd one day walked the six miles to Skipton and

72

Above: Frog in the
Middle
Right: Hot Cockles

Stilt Dance

expressed surprise that the Skipton moon was so like the one they had at Cowling.

The Redmire Feast, an important event in the Wensleydale calendar, started each year on the first Sunday after 19 September. It featured, up to about 1900, a celebration known as the Cheese-cake Gathering. The cheesecakes were in fact tarts, the size of saucers, filled with a mixture of cheese curds, eggs, butter, nutmeg and sugar. Revellers blackened their faces and wore absurd clothing for some reason lost in antiquity.

One feast celebration with a direct link with the Church was that of the Epiphany—the festival that has its origin in the Eastern Church to commemorate the baptism of Jesus, fixed at 6 January. The eating of Epiphany Cakes—known in France as *galette*—became the basis for a feast. One of the cakes contained a bean, the lucky finder being crowned the King or Queen of the Bean Feast for the following year.

Mingling of the sexes had its place at fairs and revels of the past. In 1825, William Hone wrote of seeing Kiss in the Ring being played in Greenwich Park. He believed it to be a popular game at Easter and Whitsuntide, particularly in the West Country. The young men and girls formed a ring. One boy then walked round the outside of the circle and placed a handkerchief on the shoulder of the girl of his choice who was compelled by custom to give him a kiss, but only after a chase and a show of pretended resistance. It was then the girl's turn to make her selection from the boys.

Kiss in the Ring seems an innocent enough revel activity, but there were others with a more bawdy reputation. Portsferry in Northern Ireland had an area known as the Walter. On Easter Monday the males of the community were at liberty to take hold of any girl of his choice within the limits of the Walter. The declared purpose was to give her a kiss but one does not need too much imagination to understand why Kissing at the Walter came to be condemned by the puritan element of the town's population.

Devotees of the Women's Liberation Movement may be

73

Plough Monday

surprised to know that their female ancestors had similar 'sauce for the goose' ideas. According to one reference to the Lincolnshire practice of Tutting, it was a form of orgy where 'all decency was abandoned'.

The party started with tea drinking and a little gossiping but within a short while this gave way to harder beverages. At an appointed time, a band of invited men joined the party, each putting half-a-guinea in a collecting bowl. As inhibitions receded the proceedings became less innocent. It was accepted as the ladies' night and it was permissible for them to make the advances to the men of their choice. Oh, tutt tutt!

7. Keeping Order

Market fairs of old, bringing together large numbers of traders and revellers, created problems of law enforcement. Regular police forces were unknown and the task of keeping a watchful eye on the multitude was quite beyond the local elected constables.

The itinerant merchants had their own way of enforcing justice in the form of the Court of Pie Powder which, for the duration of the fair, took over from the town watchmen, petty constables and courts leet.*

The name *pie powder* may be a corruption of *pieds poudres*, meaning 'dusty feet'—the condition in which the merchants arrived at the fair. Alternatively, it may be derived from the Old French term for a pedlar, *pied puldreaux*.

Pie Powder Courts settled disputes between traders, and saw to it that the fair was conducted in a more or less orderly manner. Above all, they took for themselves the powers of arrest and summary punishment of wrongdoers. Without the means of keeping prisoners for any period longer than the duration of the fair, justice had to be swift—fines, floggings and even hangings being the acknowledged penalties for breaking codes of behaviour.

At some fairs, notably the St Giles Fair at Winchester, a mayor and bailiff were appointed who reigned supreme for the duration of the market, administering justice, not only in Winchester, but also in Southampton and the area around, known as the *seven league circuit*.

Officials of the Court of Pie Powder had varied duties. One of the most coveted of these posts must have been the Lord of the Tap at the Stourbridge Fair. His duty was to visit all the drinking booths to make sure the ale was drinkable and up to standard.

The Court at Stourbridge was assembled at the Kings Arms, demolished only in recent times, where justice was swiftly carried out at whipping post and stocks outside. There was a strong room in the cellar, not only for the custody of offenders but for the safe keeping of cash taken at the fair.

For the Bartholomew Fair, the Court of Pie Powder was held

* A *court leet* was a court of record held in a manor house before the lord or his steward.

at a tavern called the Hand & Shears, which stood for four
centuries in Middle Street, in London's Smithfield. It was from
the door of this house that the Lord Mayor of London opened the
fair by drinking a cool tankard of wine, nutmeg and sugar. As its
name implies, this was a tavern frequented by those engaged in
the clothing trade, which was strongly represented at the Bartholomew Fair.

Keeping order at the Bartholomew Fair was an unenviable
task. Seething disquiet was never far from the surface and riots
were frequent. There was a notorious 18th century gang known
for some reason as Lady Holland's Mob, who began their riotous
activities on the eve of the opening by running through the streets,
jostling everyone they encountered and smashing the newly set
up stalls and booths. Lady Holland's Mob went too far for the
liking of the authorities when they turned to highway robbery
and were stamped out, but not before they had carved themselves
a place in the history of fairs as one of the sets of hooligans of
all time.

A Court of Pie Powder, albeit with blunted teeth, survives
to this day in at least one location: at the Stag & Hounds Inn,
Old Market Street, Bristol.

A Marching Watch   Taverns and inns were, of course, not only used as courts while the fairs were in progress. Often they accommodated the regular administration of justice. One such inn is The Bull—said to date from the 13th century—at Rolvenden, Kent, where the Justice Room is now the lounge bar. Another example is The Chequers at Sevenoaks, where there still survives a yard in which a gibbet once stood.

Although nothing to do with fairs, there were other law enforcement procedures that were continued in festival form. These were the Setting of the Watch marches that had their origins in curfews imposed by William the Conquerer. The curfew bell at 8 p.m. was the signal for the compulsory extinguishing of lights and of fires by covering the grate with a metal hood, also known as a curfew.

The official reason for the curfew was to prevent fire in the timber-built dwellings, but as the population were confined to

77

Chairing the winners
of the Dunmow Flitch

their homes and forbidden to be out on the streets from curfew until daybreak, it can be assumed that the keeping of order was an important part of the edict.

In 1103, Henry I repealed the curfew laws, an action that resulted in an increase in the incidence of murder and robbery at night. By 1253, the problem had reached such proportion that Henry III commanded that Watches be kept 'for the preservation of peace' in cities and borough towns. The Keepers of the Watch were held responsible for keeping the peace and often had to make good any losses in the event of robbery.

In the summer months, community groups would provide tables of *sweete bread* and *good drinke* for the Watches, particularly on the nights of the vigils of St John the Baptist, St Peter and St Paul. At the time of these festivals, houses were decorated with branches of birch, St John's wort, orpin and white lilies, and *bonefires* were lit.

Stowe relates that almost 2,000 men took part in the Marching Watch on St John's Eve (23 June), their numbers made up by constables as well as members of merchant companies and guilds. The procession started at Paul's Gate, passed through West-Cheape, the Stocks, Cornehill, Leadenhall, Aldgate, Fen-church street, Grasse-church, and back through the West-Cheape where the Watch broke up.

On St John's Eve in 1510, Henry VIII dressed, it is said, as a Yeoman of the guard, observed the Watch from the King's Head in the Cheape. King Christern of Denmark also saw the Watch from the same tavern in 1519.

Until 1539, when the monarch forbade the muster of armed men, there was a Marching Watch that took place annually on 8 May. In the last years of the March some 15,000 men formed up at Mile End and proceeded to Westminster, round St James and returned through Oldbourne.

An ordinance of the mayor, aldermen and common councillors of Chester, dated 1564, now preserved among the Harleian manuscripts in the British Museum, describes the Setting of the Watch in that town on St John's Eve.

It appears that it was a considerable affair, involving a procession of 'four giants, one unicorn, one dromedary, one camel, a luce [Strutt (1801) suggests this was a representation of a *flower-de-luce*], one dragon and six hobby horses'. Six naked boys ran along with the procession, beating away at the dragon with sticks.

In 1599, it is recorded, the mayor, a certain Herry Hardware (*sic*), ordered the figures of the giants to be broken up and substituted by a representation of a man in armour. However, they were not completely dismantled and, three years later the then holder of the office of mayor—a brewer by the name of John Ratcliffe—had them restored.

During the period of the Commonwealth, all the figures for the procession were destroyed, but such was the feeling of the people of Chester that, when the Restoration of Charles II presented the opportunity, the figures of the giants were replaced at the cost of £5. The bill of charges included:

Arsnick to put into the paste, to save the giants being eaten by the rats . . . one shilling and four pence.

Another place where the St John's Eve Watch was observed until the time of the Commonwealth, was Nottingham, where about 200 men assembled on The Row, carrying pikes and wearing armour.

The Marching Watches, as reasons for festivity, have long
since disappeared; they continued for a while as opening ceremonies at fairs—until 1789 in the case of the Wolverhampton
Fair, where the marchers were attired in old armour and accompanied by the music of a 'fair tune'—and modern carnival
processions to some extent reflect the tradition although other
origins, including religious processions, are involved here. At the
Topliffe Horse Fair, Yorkshire, the show of force took the form
of two men walking round the village, one carrying a pike and
the other a halberd.

There were times when the community took the law in their
own hands and, in the process of enacting justice, made something
of a revel out of the occasion. One such retributive custom was the
Ran Tan Tan—sometimes known as Riding the Stang—a
demonstration against an individual by the community.

At Willoughton, anyone who had offended the village code
was 'beaned'—beaten with fine-thonged whips and ducked in
the pond while those exacting retribution chanted a jingle, one
version of which went:

> Ran a Dan,
> Ran a Dan,
> Ran a Dan Dan.
> I ride the stang for this base hearted man.
> He ne'ar took stick, stake or star.
> But he up with his fists and knocked her o'er.

A celebration followed at the tavern.

The expression 'to give him beans', is derived from the **Ran Tan Tan**.

Another form of the Ran Tan Tan, and one of the last recorded examples of the punishment, occurred in the early 1800s in a Lincolnshire village where a schoolmaster had tied a boy to a clothes line and beaten him without mercy. Incensed, the villagers held a Ran Tan Tan on three consecutive nights, banging iron pans together and carrying an effigy of the offending teacher through the street. Outside the village the effigy was burned. The schoolmaster found employment elsewhere.

Various trades had their own methods of dealing with erring members of their fraternity. About the same time as the Ran Tan Tan practice was dying out, the bath-chairmen in the towns were punishing any colleague guilty of drunkenness, with a mock funeral. If the offending chairman did not appear at his station by 10 a.m. the 'undertaker' with his assistants would go to the man's house. The guilty one was brought out to be 'sacrificed to the jolly god', mounted on a bier and carried in procession comprising a 'sextant' with a hand bell, two 'mutes' each carrying a black stocking on a stick, and a torch bearer with a lighted lantern. When they arrived at their regular public house, the ale for the day was bought at the offender's expense.

There is some controversy about the date of origin and the founder of the court that decides on the couple to be awarded a flitch (or gammon) of bacon every fourth year at Dunmow, Essex. The two main contenders for the honour of founder are Robert, son of Richard FitzGilbert, Earl of Clare in 1111, and Robert FitzWalter some time in the reign of Henry III. In any event, the court, if it sat at all, did not make regular awards until 1751, when it is said to have been won by the surprisingly named Thomas Shakeshanks and his wife Anne!

The 'jury' at Dunmow comprise six unmarried members of both sexes. They decide on the couples to be awarded a flitch, each of whom accept the established oath:

> You shall swear by custom of confession,
> If ever you made nuptual transgression;
> Be you either married man or wife,
> By household brawls and contentious strife,
> Or otherwise in bed, or at board,
> Offend each other in deed or word;
> Or since the Parish Clerk said Amen,
> You wish't yourselves unmarried again:
> Or in a twelve months time and a day

Repented not in thought in any way:
But continued true and just in desire
As when you joined hands in the holy quire.
If to these conditions without all feare,
Of your own accord will freely sweare,
A whole gammon of bacon you will receive.
And bear it henceforth with love and good leave.
For this is our custom at Dunmow well known,
Though the pleasure is ours, the bacon's your own.

After the contestants have been 'tried', the winning couples are carried on a litter in a procession of minstrels, preceded by the flitch tied to a pole, to the church where they receive the reward . . .

A similar 'trial' used to take place at Whichoure, Staffordshire, where bacon and corn were awarded to the harmonious couple.

The authenticity of the Dunmow Flitch trial must be a matter for speculation, but what matter? It remains a source of merry-making in an age when local and home-cured entertainment is rare.

8. Blessings, Dressings and Garlands

A Wodehouse

A Green Man

Festivals involving the blessing of produce or the means of livelihood have their origins in pagan sacrificial ceremonies. They survived the adoption of Christianity and often gained an overlay of Church approval, but the pagan and sometimes barbaric roots are not far from the surface. Almost invariably the rites are accompanied or preceded by feasting and merrymaking.

A few blessing ceremonies survive to this day, a typical example being the Blessing of the Mead in August at Gulval, St Mounts Bay, Cornwall. St Bartholomew being the patron saint of bee-keepers and honey makers, the blessing is carried out by the Almoner of the Fraternity of St Bartholomew, an officer of the Craft, or Mystery, of Free Meadmakers of Great Britain and Ireland.

At Abbotsbury, Dorset, each year on 13 May, the fishing boats of the port were blessed. Garlands of flowers were arranged by children into time-honoured shapes, taken out to sea and cast adrift. Garlands are still made but are now placed on the town's war memorial.

Similarly, the last Friday in October marks the Oyster Festival at Colchester, Essex. The mayor goes out in one of the oyster boats and makes the first dredge of the season. A loyal toast is drunk in gin, and gingerbread is eaten.

Celebrations connected with the plough and fertility of the earth were enacted on several days in the early weeks of January in a ritualistic offering to the forces of nature in the hope of a good harvest in the coming year.

Plough Monday itself, the date around which the celebrations are centred, falls on the first Monday after Twelfth Night. In some places the day was marked by a procession of thirty or forty ribbon bedecked men driving a plough, accompanied by a 'fool' and a 'bessie'—an old woman character dressed in skins, who collected money from the bystanders to be spent later in merry-making. In Norfolk the ceremony had a minimal ecclesiastic approval in that churches had 'plough lights' showing through the Sunday night and Monday morning. Plough blessing cele-brations survive in places in the counties of Devon, Norfolk and Essex.

Right: Garland Day at Castleton

Left: Oyster Festival at Colne
Below left: Blessing the Fishing Boats at Folkestone

Apple Wassailing at Carhampton

At Pauntley, on the borders of Gloucestershire and Worcestershire, farmers had their celebrations in a field marked down for growing wheat in the coming year. A row of fires were lit, one larger than the others. Round this they drank cider and toasted the future harvest. When the fires died down the farmers returned to the village to continue drinking cider containing, for some obscure reason, carraway seeds.

Often Plough Jags were rough and threatening affairs. In parts of Lincolnshire on Plough Monday, law enforcement was relaxed to permit the jag. A gang of plough boys, two-abreast and trailing a wooden plough, was driven along the village streets by a lad wielding a long whip. Each house was visited and if no money was forthcoming, the front path was ploughed up. Cash, so gained, later found its inevitable way into the ale-house keeper's pocket. In some places a small anchor, known as a *stot*, was used in place of a plough.

Allied with the plough celebrations was the wassailing of the apple orchards in the western counties of England. 'Was-haile' and 'Drinc-heil' were the customary quaffing phrases used in medieval times, in the same way 'Come, here's to you' and 'I pledge thee', were used in the 18th and 19th centuries, replaced by 'Cheers' and 'Bottoms up' in more recent times.

Legend has it that the origin of the early greeting is owed to Rowena, daughter of the Saxon, Hengist, when welcoming the

Young and old
preparing well dressings,
Derbyshire

British king, Voltigern, with wine and the words, 'Louerd King, Wass-heil', to which Voltigern replied, 'Drinc-heil'.

Wassailing in the apple orchards was performed through the twelve days of Christmas. Each tree was toasted with cider, after which a shot was fired into the tree—something like a kiss and a threat to encourage a bumper crop in the coming year. The wassailing of the trees was often performed on Christmas Eve, but at Carhampton, Somerset, the ceremony took place on Old Twelfth Night. In this particular version, the largest tree was selected, round it a circle was formed by the villagers chanting an incarnation to keep away the evil spirits capable of causing the dreaded blight. Shots were then fired into the trees and the participants returned to the village to drink to the forthcoming harvest.

> A massy bowl, to deck the jovial day,
> Flash'd from its ample round a sunlike ray,
> Full many a century it shon forth to grace
> The festive spirit of the Andarton race.
> As, to the sons of sacred union dear,
> It welcomed with lambs wool* the rising tear.
>
> Devon poem by Polwhele.

* Lambs wool was a drink of spiced ale or cider.

86

Before the advent of piped water, the well was symbolic of a means to maintain life, and the dressing of wells with flowers and gifts as a thanksgiving was once an important part of the Spring calendar throughout Britain. The celebration still survives in a number of places but as a mere picturesque shadow of the past.

Not only wells were ceremoniously dressed. During the Grassington Feast, an important revel in the 18th century, invitations were sent out suggesting to guests that they 'come and dress the clock'. The origin of this particular type of celebration is not known, nor is the nature of the merrymaking as no records survive.

Thanksgiving seems to be the motive behind ceremonial Rush Bearing which originated in the days when the floors of homes and churches were of earth and it was necessary to make a covering with rushes and straw.

There is a Rush Bearing ceremony at Grasmere, Westmorland (now Cumbria) on the Saturday nearest to St Oswald's Day (9th August) and another on Whit Sunday at St Mary Redcliffe, Bristol. The latter is said to date from 1493 when the mayor, one William Spenser, left a bequest for the church to be strewn with rushes and flowers, and for three sermons to be preached in the presence of the current mayor.

The churchyard at Painswick, Gloucester, contains ninety-nine yew trees—the hundredth has always failed to grow. On the Sunday following 19 September (The Nativity of Our Lady), the church is 'clipped' or embraced by children holding hands

Rush Laying at St Mary Redcliffe
Right: Church Clipping at Painswick

and dancing round the church, in and out of the yew trees, and singing a special Clipping Hymn. After the ceremony the villagers partake of Puppy-Dog Pie which, in recent years, has been modified to a cake containing a china dog.

Similar ceremonies take place at Wirksworth and Burbage, Derbyshire, the former in September and the latter in July.

Perhaps allied with Church Clipping is the ceremony at Lanark on 1 March, called Whuppity Scoorie, during which children parade round the parish church swinging paper balls.

There seems no limit to the things that have been dressed with flowers: wells, clocks, church floors and even stools. In Northumberland, up to the early 19th century, stools were dressed with flowers set in clay and placed at the ends of streets. It was a form of begging to pay for the merrymaking ale—the streets competing with each other for the most attractive display.

Floral garlands are strongly associated with May Day, a hangover from the Roman Festival of Floralia. At Randwich, near Stroud, Gloucester, cheeses were the subjects to be bedecked

Barnet Horse Fair

with garlands up to the mid-19th century. Three large cheeses were decorated, placed on litters and carried through the village with accompanying music. On arrival at the churchyard, the cheeses were rolled three times round the church.

Chimney sweeps and milkmaids in London were two groups who used garlands as part of their May Day celebration. The sweeps' garland was a large cone of holly and ivy formed from hoops of various sizes, carried by a man inside. Sweeps, dressed in their best clothes, danced round collecting from passers-by.

The milkmaids also used May Day as an excuse to solicit donations; their garland was more feminine, comprising a tall pyramid and covered with a white cloth and decorated with silver and ribbons.

Yet another May Day garland celebration to the goddess Flora was held at Lynn, Norfolk. The garland was formed from two hoops fixed transversely and attached to a pole. It was decorated with flowers, ribbons and blown birds' eggs tied to the hoops and topped with a doll to represent the goddess. The work was that of the inmates of the St James workhouse, which benefited from the collection made during the procession round the town. It is claimed that the celebration originated from the time when the Roman colony held their Festival of Floralia. It was banned in 1644, the year when the merrymaking had to stop by order of the Protector—but was reintroduced in 1682.

9. *The Showman's Fair*

A Tumbler

The 18th century brought about changes in the nature of fairs. The distribution of goods from manufacturers to shops was becoming more efficient and, as the century progressed there was less trading and more emphasis on amusements: peepshows, rope walkers, freak shows, and the first of the 'rides': swing boats, whirligigs (merry-go-rounds), and the up and down (big wheel). There was, of course, no convenient source of power, and the rides depended on man or woman power, absorbed by treadmill or crank.

The style of the barkers' cries were changing. 'Cheap John's here the day', was giving way to 'Come to the great Tom Matthews Show'.

At the Clack Fair, a merryandrew by the name of Joe Ody, obtained permission from the Court of Pie Powder to 'show forth by conjuring rings off women's fingers, and finding them in men's pockets, eating fire and drawing yards of ribbons out of his mouth, giving shuffling tricks with cards, to ascertain how much money was in a ploughman's yellow purse, cutting off cocks' heads, pricking in the garter for love tokens, giving a chance on the black cock or the white cock, and lastly, raising the devil, who carries off the cheating parish baker upon his back'—all typical 18th century showman's fair attractions.

Also at the Clack Fair performed a 'learned dog, dancing bears, monkeys with three dogs, all in red jackets with pipes in their mouths, and a climbing cat which climbed a pole and returned to its box on command'.

Performing dogs were ever-popular attractions. At the Southwark Fair in the 18th century, a showman by the name of Crawley presented his show billed as The Ball of Little Dogs. It was claimed that the dogs came from Louvain and had been taught to perform 'by cunning tricks, wonders in the world of dancing. . . . You shall see one of them, named Gaillerdain (the frisky one), whose dexterity is not to be compared; he dances with madame Poncette his mistress and the rest of their company at the sounds of instruments, all of them observing so well the cadence, that they amaze every body.' Crawley declared that his dogs had danced before Queen Anne.

Trained Dog

Another famous troupe of dogs, this time in the early 19th century, performed at Sadler's Wells and at Astley's Circus. One dog, acting the part of a lady, was carried by two other dogs. In another act the dogs sat at table and were waited upon. The concluding act was an attack on a fort by the entire troupe.

Astley's Circus in London's Westminster Bridge Road, the enterprise of an ex-soldier, was established in 1770, as the first collective spectacle of wandering animal trainers, acrobats, rope walkers and like brethren who until then were seen only at fairs.

A visitor to a 19th century fair would find booths selling 'fine and fat oysters', fruit, cheap toys, wicker baskets, wood-cut pamphlets, bible prints, garters, gingerbread—with prices ranging between ½d and half a sovereign.

Bars and eating places abounded, carrying the signs in gaudy profusion: The Brighton Pavilion, The Royal Eating Room, Fair Rosamund's Bower, New London Tavern and The Imperial Hotel. At these temporary establishments, one could dine handsomely for 3d and sumptuously for 4d.

At the 'Only A Penny' peepshow, the visitor could peer through a magnifying glass while the showman pulled down a series of canvas screens, each graphically depicting a subject of

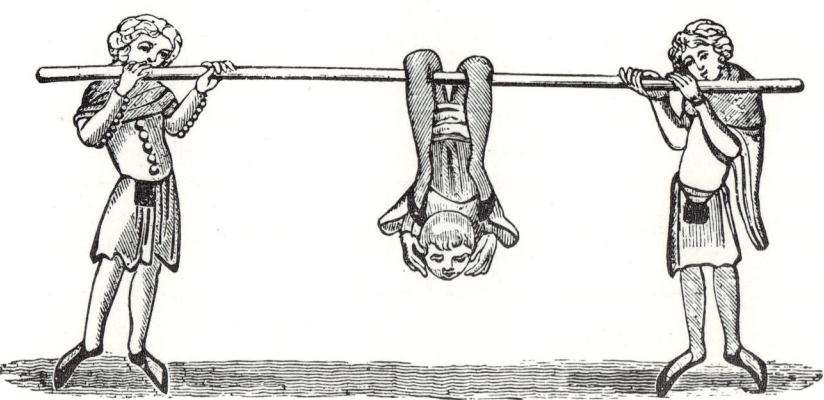

A Posture Master

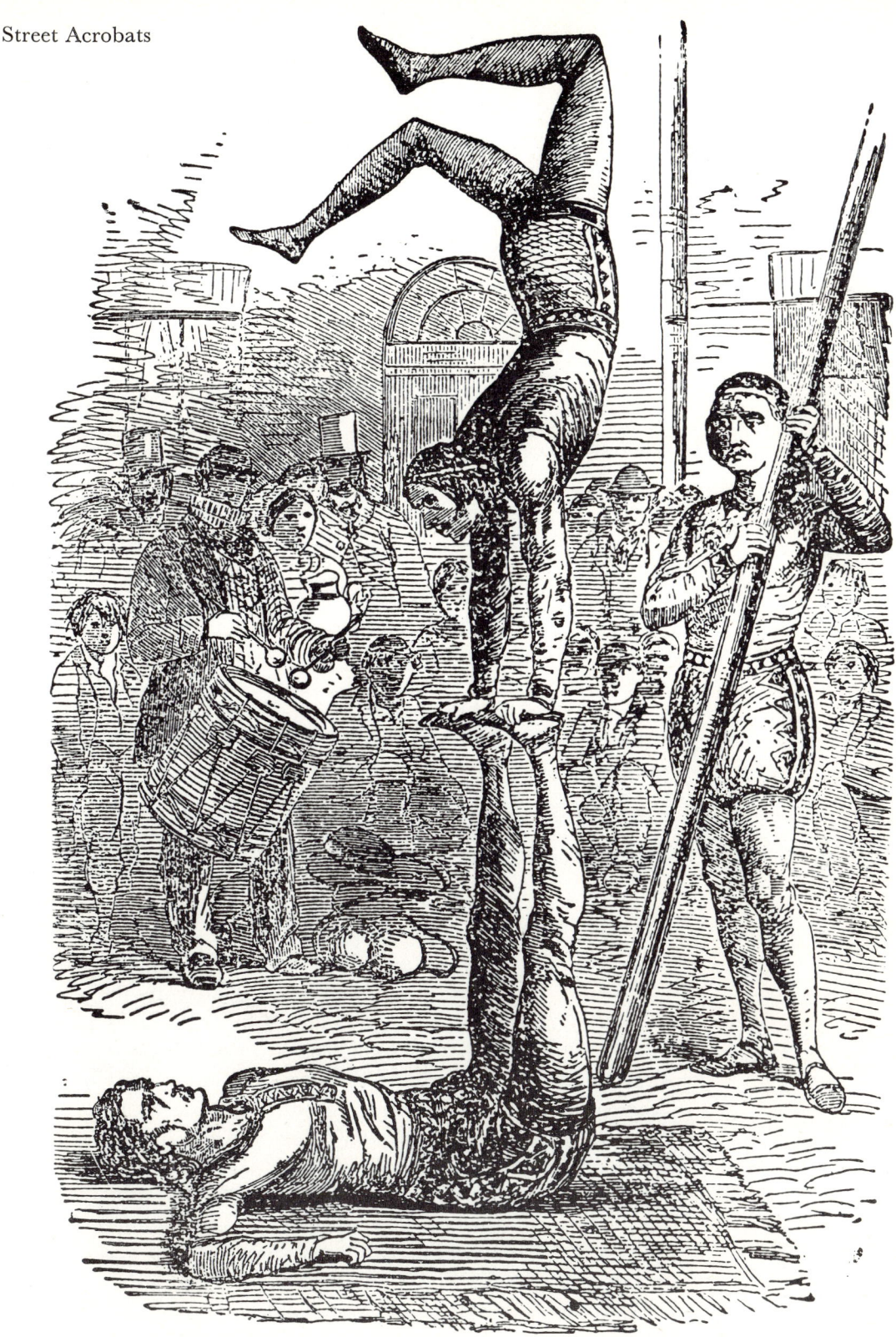

the type expected by the people of the time: The Murder of Mr Weare and Probert's Cottage, Execution of William Probert, The Visit of the Queen of Sheba to King Solomon on the Throne, Daniel in the Den of Lions, St Paul's Cathedral, The Tower of Babel, The Greenland Whale Fishery, Battle of Waterloo, A View of the City of Dublin and The Coronation of George IV. Other peepshows displayed less decorum and taste.

Drama, both sensational and bible-inspired, had its place in the repertoire of the bands of travelling actors. A scene from *The Cruelty of Artreus* performed at the Bartholomew was described thus: 'the scene wherein Thyestes eats his own children is to be performed by the famous Mr Psalmanazar, lately arrived from Formosa, the whole supper being set to kettle drums'.

Freak shows were popular. Here could be viewed Miss Hipson

the Middlesex Wonder—the Largest Child in the Kingdom, The Persian Giant, The Fair Negro with Silver Hair, The Female Dwarf—Two Feet Eleven Inches High, or The Wild Indian from the Malay Islands of the East, who could say 'a drop a' rum' with great glee. There was a ventriloquist 'who talks in his belly and can fling his voice into any part of the room'.

If tastes extended to the wonders of the animal kingdom, the competitive draw was Atkin's Royal Menagerie, housing a mare with five feet, and a beast described as an *aurochus*. One of the best known travelling collections of wild animals in the early 19th century was Wombwell's Menagerie. It was at the Hull Fair that the last of the Wombwells met his death from a mauling from one of his lions. Accidents with wild animals were common. Revellers were more concerned with enjoying themselves than with safety. At the Lynn Valentine Fair in Norfolk in 1796, a

Minstrels

95

man lost his arm when he was foolish enough to put it in a lion's mouth.

Prices of admission to freak shows and menageries were remarkably high. Even as long ago as 1830, one had to pay a shilling for an adult and six pence for a child. However, for this sum another wonder of the age could be observed at the same time—gas lighting illuminating the show.

The true showman did not necessarily need the elaborate and costly exhibition to attract people. In the 1820s there was a travelling gypsy showman called Old Corey Dyne. His booth was simply an old hat, upside down on the ground, with a stake

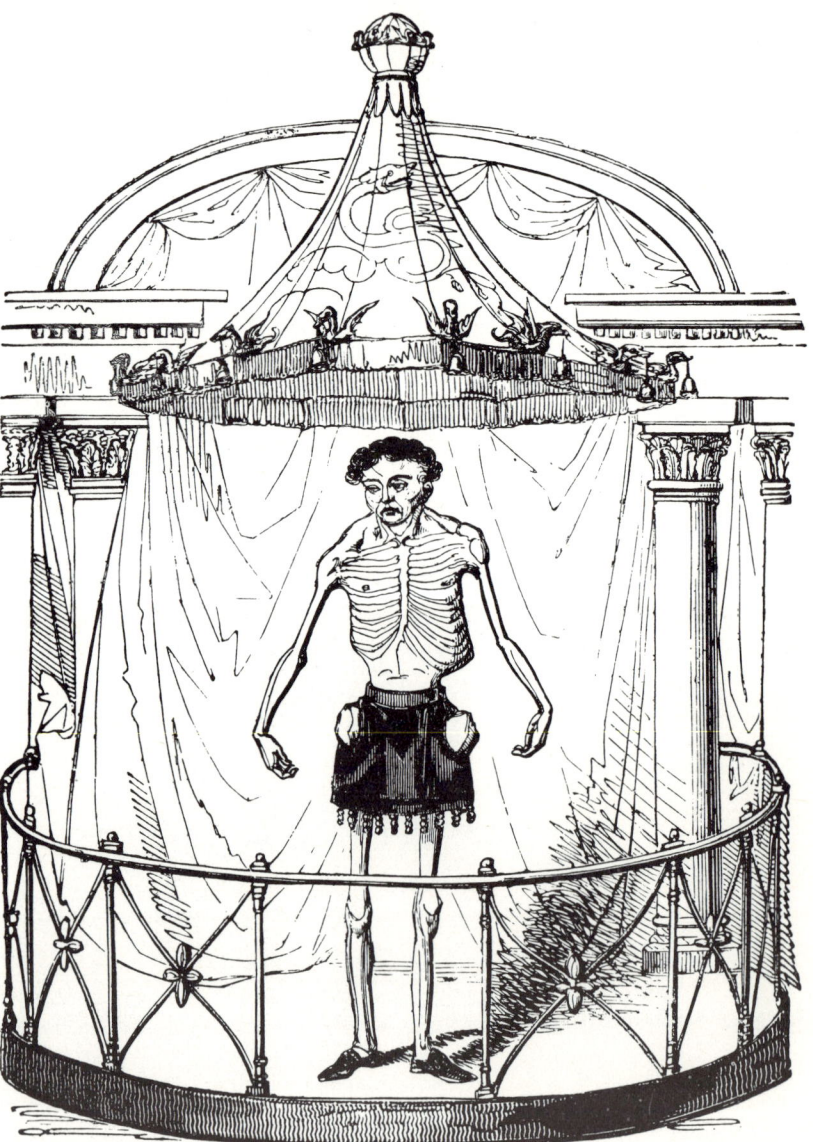

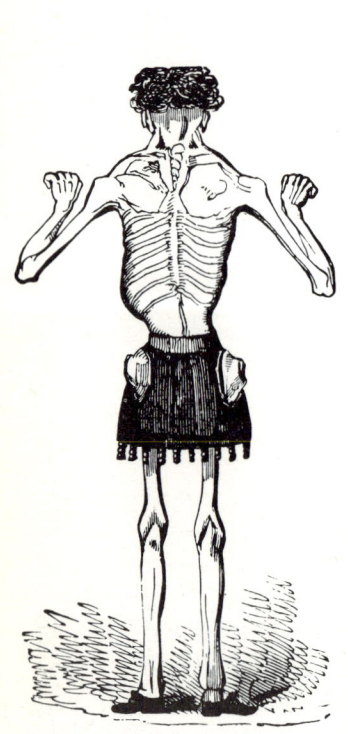

The Living Skeleton

driven through it. On the top of the stake rested a halfpenny
which challengers had to knock off with wooden balls. If the
coin fell outside the hat he was awarded a prize. Old Corey
Dyne died a rich man after 50 years on the road.

Mr Merryman—a very merry fellow, it is said—needed no
equipment at all. After collecting a few contributions 'to clear
the throat', he proceeded to give his bird impressions: nightin-
gales, blackbirds, linnets, goldfinches, robins, geese, ducks,
turkeys—any bird the punters called for. Mr Merryman's
favourite venue was the Purton Fair in Wiltshire, opened on
3 September with pleasure as the principal aim. It is said that the
local tavern sold over 6,000 gallons of ale through the three
days of the fair in the 1820s. The Purton Fair was famous for its
singlestick fight between men of Purton and those from nearby
Stretton, and for a cricket match between 20-men-strong teams
from the villages.

Some of the sideshows were not so agreeable as Mr Merryman.
On a researching visit to Boston in Lincolnshire, the author was
told by a very elderly gentleman, over a pint, of a particularly
horrid show called The Rat Girl—a young woman sitting in a
cage with rats crawling all over her. Boston used to have two
annual fairs: The Beast Fair and the Bull Fair. The former
opening on 3 May for a week; as it closed, so the Bull Fair opened.

There is a multitude of variations on the theme of the game
where the thrower of a well-aimed missile is rewarded. The
coconut shy is considered the most traditional, but the Aunt

Sideshow at the
Bartholomew Fair

Sally is certainly older, having a common root with the tavern game of the same name.

Throwing at Pyramids of Cans, Crockery Smash and Knocking Off the Top Hat are based on the old fair stall attraction of Jack in The Box in which the object was to hit the man who popped his head out of the box at irregular intervals.

There still survives Tipping the Bucket—with an element of the tournament sport of Quintain—the object being to hit a target when a bucket of water is tipped over a young woman, usually attired in a swim suit. This is a more common side show at local fêtes than at commercial fairs, with the girl a willing volunteer to suffer in the cause of sweet charity. A derivative of this is Tipping the Girl Out of Bed; at this stall a girl is lying on a bed and when the target is struck, the bed tips up to roll the girl from her slumbers.

Water Tub Quintain
Right: Early Swing

98

One Man Band
Right: A Peep Show

Tutored Bears

Fairs were a happy hunting ground for tricksters. In Kelly's *History of Drama in Leicester* is quoted a prosecution case of 1794, when 'one, Richardson, and others, sharpers, for playing at a game called *Pricking in the Old Hat*'. Kelly assumed the game to be similar to Pricking at the Belt or Girdle, also called Fast and Loose, mentioned by Brand in *Popular Antiquities* as being much practised by gypsies in the days of Shakespeare. The punter was challenged to push a pin through a folded cloth belt so as to anchor it to the table. After a few dummy runs, the operator folded the belt in such a way as to make it impossible to win.

Allied tricks were Find the Lady, and Thimble and Pea, both of which can still be seen on the streets of London with the operator keeping furtive watch for the police.

The travelling showmen were never slow to grasp a chance to set up a fair. On Sunday, 30 January 1814, the river Thames

99

Fantoccini, the ancester of Punch and Judy

froze solid. By the afternoon of the following day, hundreds of Londoners had assembled on the ice between London Bridge and Blackfriars. By noon on Tuesday, traders and showmen were taking advantage of the situation and providing entertainment. Sixpence was demanded for witnessing the spectacle of roasting a sheep on the ice, the 'Lapland Mutton' being sold at one shilling a slice. The inevitable gin, beer and gingerbread booths were set up, and the first of the several Thames Frost Fairs of the 19th century had begun.

100

Some printing presses were established on the ice, publishing souvenirs. One sheet ran:

Frost Fair
Amidst the arts which on the Thames appear,
To tell the wonders of this icey year.
Printing claims prior place, which at one view
Erects a monument of That and You.

It was more like a rural summer revel than a busy city in mid-winter: swings, bookstalls, dancing, skittle alleys, donkey rides, and gambling booths where Londoners could place their bets on E-O (Even-Odd) a roulette style of game with which Beau Nash had tempted the water cure seekers of Bath and Tunbridge Wells years before, Rouge et Noir, Teetotum, and the Wheel of Fortune.

A German Showman

On Thursday evening the ice began to melt and crack. Much of the vendors' and showmen's equipment was irretrievably lost and there was also some loss of life. However the indomitable showmen salvaged what they could and set off for the next fair.

Born and bred to weather vicissitudes which would soon defeat a less resilient community, the travelling showmen only know one way to survive.

Epilogue

The Changing Face of the Fair

Brenda Kidman

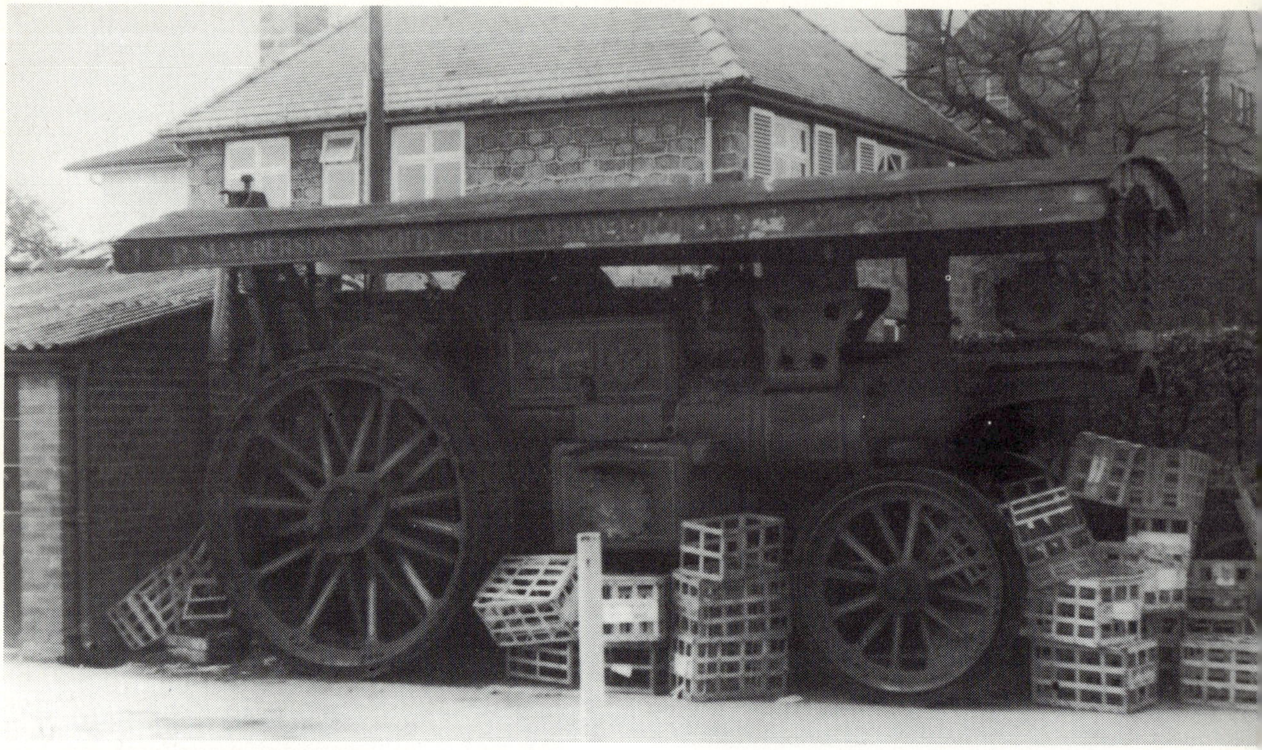

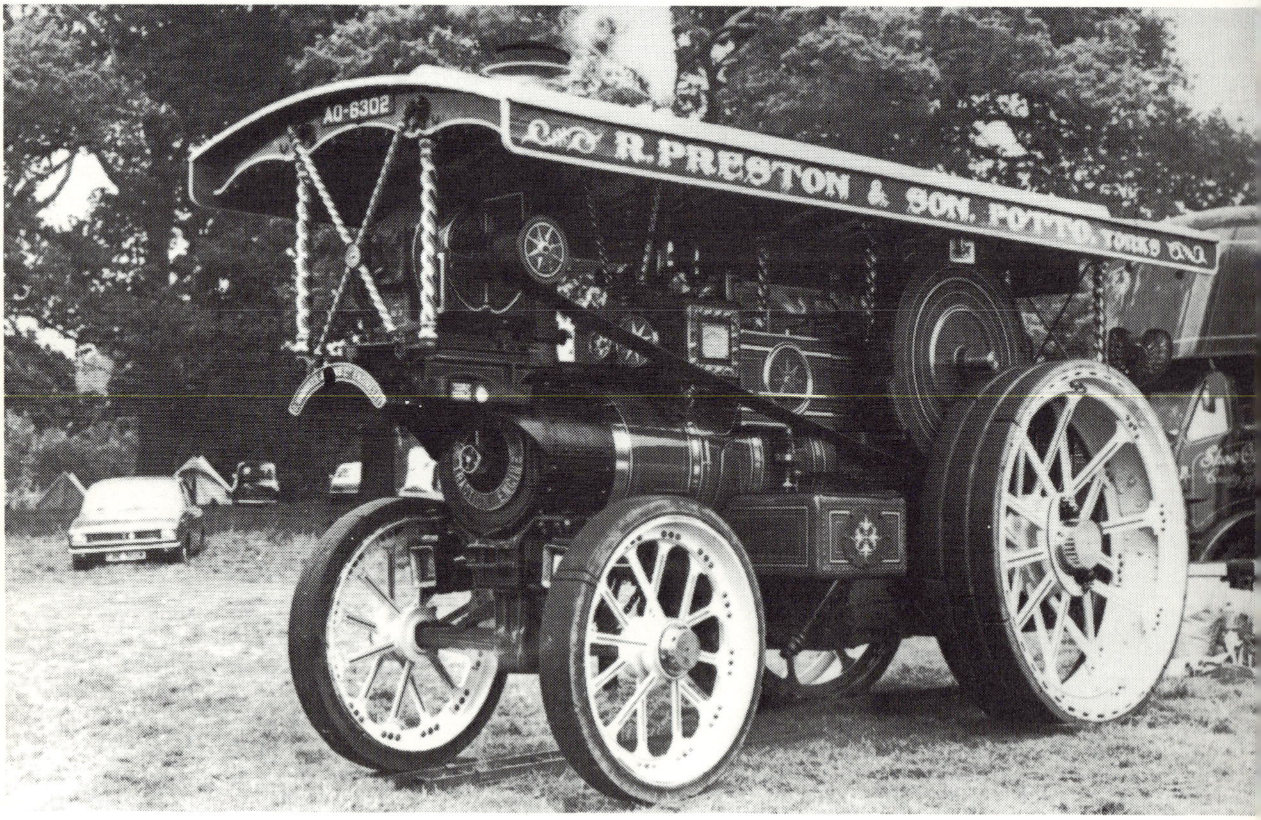
AO-6302
R. PRESTON & SON. POTTO. YORKS

The Changing Face of the Fair

Fairs and revels, highdays and holidays, these were the traditional forms of merry-making which ancient charters entitled every citizen the right to enjoy. They also granted itinerant entertainers the right to provide them, to pursue a nomadic way of life on the fringes of contemporary society which they still do to this day. To what extent we value the vital place they occupy in our folk heritage—whether indeed we value it at all—is what we intend to explore on the following pages.

A century ago working people had a limited choice of cheap and cheerful entertainment. Townsfolk had the Music Hall and the fairground, countrymen had to settle for Hobson's choice—just the fair. Undoubtedly this was a restriction which greatly increased their appreciation of it and country people were known to save from one year to the next for the arrival of the travelling showmen. On the Victorian fairground sixpence bought all the fun of the fair and with a shilling in his pocket the fortunate reveller could purchase food and drink besides.

Today's comparatively affluent citizen enjoys mobility, paid holidays and a wide variety of recreations. Consequently his attitude towards the travelling funfair varies from indifference to thinly veiled hostility. Some complain that fairs constitute a nuisance by increasing congestion in built-up areas, attract rowdy elements and pollute the environment with noise and litter. All too often urban council redevelopment schemes appear to endorse this attitude. Old fairground sites become carparks and supermarkets, fairs are pushed to the outskirts of towns where not only is the soft ground unsuitable for heavy equipment but the showmen are obliged to compete at a distance with firmly entrenched city centre amusements.

These then are some of the external pressures which threaten the future of the travelling people. Unfortunately they are by no means the complete picture.

Today travelling funfairs not only face running costs which rocket faster than the latest space-age rides but rules and regulations which complicate their lives out of all recognition. Fairground historians cite steam and electricity as the revolu-

Top:
Scenic Burrell No. 4030.
Built 1925 for Wm
Davis Amusements. Seen
here derelict in 1973
Bottom:
Burrell No. 3526.
Originally built for
Emerson & Hazard
of Whitehaven in 1913

89 Key Gavioli Organ. Owned by L. Cole of Leeds, this organ was imported to England from Apeldoorn in Holland

tionary developments which transformed the old-time fairground to the benefit of all concerned. In fact they also set in motion a train of events which did much more than change the face of the fair.

Between 1870 and 1900 showmen were quick to appreciate the advantages of steam traction and eagerly hitched this powerful energy star to their wagons. Hand-cranked or horse-propelled roundabouts were relegated to the realms of antiquity and the travelling people set off on a new era of mechanisation.

By harnessing steam as a means of stationary propulsion now showmen could invest in much larger and more elaborate pleasure machines. Built mostly by Savages of King's Lynn, some of the most famous rides ever to grace the fairground appeared at this time. The romantic, gilded three-abreast Gallopers, Scenic Railways, Steam Yachts and Switchbacks, each one supplied to the showmen complete with steam traction engine, water-dandy and flat trucks for transporting these mammoth roundabouts from one fair to the next.

Of course this equipment involved the showmen in tremendous capital outlay but even on halfpenny and penny rides they more

3-a-breast Gallopers, extensively restored by A. Corrigan of Scarborough. They are now electrically driven and the organ is a dummy replica playing taped music. The Gallopers are now owned by G. Warrington and situated at a zoo in North Yorkshire

than recouped their investments. Extending credit to unskilled and largely illiterate showmen, Frederick Savage had remarkably few defaulters.

Chugging valiantly about the countryside at 5 mph, steam traction engines hauled the showmen's seven and eight truck road trains efficiently and quickly. Showmen who dismantled their tackle one night could, twenty-four hours later, appear at a fair ninety miles away, a journey which would previously have taken them several days. All the same, steam engines were not all plain sailing. On every steep hill the showmen had to uncouple the trucks at the bottom and then, driving the steam engine to the summit, separately winch each trailer up behind. These road trains, as showmen's linked trucks and trailers are still called to this day, often weighed close on forty tons exclusive of the family living van. Nevertheless it was spectacular mobility and even prompted a degree of one-upmanship for the steam traction owner able to steal a march on his horse-drawn colleagues to commandeer the best pitch at the next fairground!

As a veteran driver of the day remarked: 'If you were going down a country lane on a steam engine and ran out of coke, you

Cake Walk owned by
L. Bishton. This Ride
still travels to many
Fairs and Rallies. Mr
Bishton has retained the
original owner's name
on the front

could always go in the woods for an armful of kindling—even put
your hat on the fire. With tired horses you were plain stuck!'

But if steam began the acceleration of the fairground scene, it
was electricity which sparked off a whole new era of automation.
Here was an entirely new source of energy and the showmen did
not hesitate to exploit it, adding the skill of electrician to their
already impressive list of personal accomplishments.

Victorian punters, previously showered by black smuts from
naptha flares, were enthralled by the garish but clean illumina-
tions which transformed the fairgrounds in the early 1900s.
Showmen, often faced with the hazardous night operation of dis-
mantling heavy equipment, could now safely illuminate their
work. Electricity also powered the famous Bioscope shows, crude
prototypes of the modern cinema, originally popularised at fairs.

In those days people seldom ventured far from home so the
enterprising showmen took moving pictures to the people. Upon
arrival in a new town they often went out into the streets to film
local inhabitants, thus ensuring that if patrons were not especially
attracted by a programme which included such epics as *The
Performing Flea* or *The Perils of Pauline*, they would part gladly with
threepence for a chance to see themselves on the screen.

The Bioscopes—or Electrographs as some were called—proved
immensely profitable. In the tent behind the show front there was

often seating for five hundred with standing room for just as many. Fairground customers who declined to go inside could still enjoy a marvellous free show outside where, framed by flashing lights and the elaborately gilded and carved proscenium, dancing girls pranced to the music of mechanical trumpet organs. But by 1914 permanently sited picture palaces sprung up on every high street and the glorious reign of the fairground Bioscope was over.

Having pioneered the development of the early cinema the showmen now found it had become their principal entertainment rival. Characteristically resilient, they felt confident that what had —so to speak—been lost on the swings would soon be gained on the roundabouts. Edwardians still loved their fairs and the showmen were sure that on the fairground they had an infallible recipe for success—entertainment with universal appeal. In fact they probably provided a lot more. In the guise of amusements, the showmen created an outdoor arena where at one and the same time the working man could harmlessly satisfy his competitive and gambling instincts, his curiosity, his craving for the illusion of free flight and—when necessary—also express his frustrations and aggressions. In their way the showmen were primitive psychologists with a shrewd insight into human nature. They were also expert at exploiting this insight to their own financial advantage! Naturally the showmen's tackle sometimes suffered in the process, but this was all part and parcel of their business.

Another Cake Walk which up to a few years ago was travelled by a Showman called Bishton. It is now thought to have been sold

Travelling from industrial to dockland areas in the early 1900s, fairgrounds were often the scene for rowdyism—even gang warfare —and once the public houses closed they were frequently invaded by drunks. There's many a showman of the day who recalls washing the blood from his ride before packing up to move off again.

These were rough, tough times for the showmen but at least the fairground was thriving. During the years which followed, even the ingenious showmen were hard-pressed to survive.

After World War 1 enlisted showmen returned to find the social scene completely altered. Familiar with all forms of mechanisation in their every day lives, now the public could easily indulge in such diversions as radio, motor-racing, cinemas, amusement parks and sports facilities. Always ready to translate competition into a challenge, the showmen did their best to devise new ways to resuscitate the fairground but before they could properly do so found themselves enveloped by the economic depression which led to the General Strike of 1926.

Funfairs continued to travel and, if nothing else, managed to bring a little light relief to the lives of the unemployed masses,

B. Crow's Speedway. Built 1937. Pictured here at Darlington in 1976

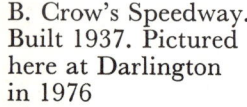

although sometimes it was necessary to entice customers onto the fairground by offers of free food. More than one showman of that day remembers presenting every roundabout patron with a bar of nougat!

During this period many showmen became bankrupt and, in order to lend fresh impetus to the business, the others had to invest heavily in newly developed equipment. So, in 1928, Dodgems made their first appearance on fairgrounds and once again the perspicacious showmen had scored a winner.

Just as patrons at the turn of the century had enjoyed the sensation of speed riding on the gently gyrating ostriches and camels of the old scenic rides so the next generation thrilled to the excitement of being able to manipulate 'their own motor cars'. Another sensational attraction on fairgrounds at that time was The Wall of Death and the spectacle of daredevil motorcyclists apparently defying gravity was immensely popular. All the same it was riding devices such as these which finally brought the fairground under the watchful eye of the Home Office and in order to operate what was potentially dangerous equipment, the showmen had to be insured. They were also subjected to inspec-

101 Key Mortier Dance Organ, built 1928 in Antwerp. Originally used in a dance hall. Imported into England in 1962 by the late David Barlow

tion by local officials from the fire department, the council and the police who were concerned that no fair should be allowed to open until all the regulations concerning public safety had been meticulously observed. Inevitably there were also other interferences which affected the showmen.

Humane concerns such as the RSPCA and NSPCC managed to abolish the exhibition of live animal and human freaks; the Lord's Day Observance societies stopped fairs opening on Sundays and school inspectors started to tighten up on the showmen's casual attitude to education for their children. Inexorably the showmen's independent lifestyle was coming under the watchful jurisdiction of authority and when, in the late 1930s, they were just beginning to enjoy some kind of financial recovery, war was declared.

Overnight all forms of amusement ceased and, abandoning their tackle, the showmen enlisted. Fairground steam engines were commandeered for the war effort—for agricultural purposes and during the Blitz for demolition—and government scrap metal drives for armaments not only ripped out railings from one end of the land to the other, but also collected many derelict fairground rides.

89 Key Gavioli Organ, built 1909 used with Sidney White's Electric Coliseum Bioscope Show (it was then 112 Key). The show was six times larger than the organ

Showman Harry Lee
pictured with his
Steam Yachts at Boston
May Fair

In 1945 demobbed showmen hurried back to their yards hoping to refurbish their amusements in time to contribute to the VE and VJ celebrations. War-weary citizens longed for any form of amusement but the showmen's usually indomitable resourcefulness could do nothing to combat the acute shortage of timber, canvas, paint and fuel. Some patched up their tackle and took to the road again; others, thoroughly unsettled by the war years, left the business.

It was during the immediate post-war period that countless steam-driven rides and mechanical organs were junked. Usually able to remain one jump ahead of public taste, this time the showmen seriously miscalculated. They could not envisage a time when such out-dated equipment would ever again be wanted by a speed-crazy public. There was one showman who obstinately refused to subscribe to this belief and continued to travel with a splendid old ride called The Steam Yachts, built by Frederick Savage's in 1900 to commemorate the Trans-Atlantic yacht race which featured the British boat, *Shamrock*, and the American boat, *Columbia*.

Although four years in an open yard had severely damaged the Yachts, Harry Lee restored them down to the last detail and subsequently operated them in their original form, with central steam engine to propel the two giant swing-boats and belt-drive the Chiappa organ on the front. He even retained his traditional-style living wagon for himself and his wife, his only concession to modernity a war-surplus diesel tractor to haul the 87 feet road train—at an average speed of 12 mph!

Other showmen were investing heavily in the ultra-modern fibre-glass and steel rides which made their first appearance at the Festival of Britain at Battersea in 1950, leaving Harry Lee—as they thought—to gently fade away, while they spun off into the space-age technology which exists on today's fairground.

Nevertheless, today's funfair showmen are no technocrats in high-rise offices. Behind the bright lights of the fairground they lead a domestic existence which is now an odd combination of stoicism and self-indulgence—with one predominating ingredient: total commitment to family unity.

Born and bred on the fairground, many families can claim an unbroken lineage which goes back two and even three hundred years. Amongst travelling people divorce is uncommon, their alfresco lifestyle makes them exceptionally healthy, and retirement is not a word which features in their vocabulary.

A close-knit and entirely self-sufficient community, inevitably there are few families which cannot—one way or another—claim connections, although this kinship is sometimes intricate.

113

'My grandmother and his mother were sisters so he was my mother's own cousin...' was the relationship Violet Hibble claimed with her husband Morny Mellor, in their day a familiar duo on the Midland circuit. And whether or not they are distantly related, many families can within their structure claim allegiance to a variety of counties. A family of five had this to say:

'I come from Gloucestershire, my husband was born in Yorkshire, our eldest was born in Kent, the second in Lincolnshire and the last in Nottinghamshire...'

Showmen's children seldom marry outside the business and although it might be over-cynical to suggest that such a romantic alliance is impossible, it would also be fair to say that no *Ride Master* would encourage his son and heir to dally with the daughter of a *joint* owner!

On the fairground there has always existed the *elitism* of ownership. Those with the large mechanical rides dominate the centre of the fair whilst the booths and *joints* (stalls) are satellites on the perimeter. Handing down their giant toys, father to son, Ride Masters are comparable to Lords of the Manor, the difference being that one bequeaths his inherited livelihood, the other his estates.

3-a-breast Gallopers. This Ride is travelled by Screeton Bros of Barton upon Humber. It can be seen most times steam driven, a new Savage centre engine having been installed at the start of the 1976 season. The **Ride** has an 89 key Gavioli Organ installed

G. Eddy & Sons
Dodgem loads seen here
on the M62 Motorway
near Leeds, heading for
Askern. The Eddys have
two Atkinson Vehicles
used with the Dodgems;
the other lorry carries
the nets and plates and
pulls the living wagon.
This picture was taken
6th March 1976—the
Eddys' first trip after
the winter lay-up in
Leeds

Nor is liberation a new word on the fairground. Men and women have always been equal business partners for the very practical reason that neither could survive without the other. Children, too, learn early to take on some of the responsibilities which go to make up what is essentially a family enterprise, and despite the perennial romanticising of poets and playwrights looking no further than the bright lights of the fairground for their sentimental impression of it, behind those colourful façades the life of the travelling people is more often than not both repetitive and arduous. Showmen may well be the *fly-by-nights* of the amusement world but a fair isn't a magical happening! It is the result of carefully co-ordinated gatherings of largely un-co-ordinated units which, if for no other reason than this, deserve to be preserved as an intriguing and unique part of our welfare society.

In the past, memorising the dates and places which entitled them to present their amusements, showmen perigrinated haphazardly. If three coconut shies turned up at the same fair and tried to do business within spitting distance of one another, those concerned made the best of it. Probably the *barker* with the most amusing *spiel* would attract the customers in days when the human

115

voice on the fairground was not drowned out by amplified music. Nowadays, armed with a comprehensive list of each and every fair due to take place, while still in Winter Quarters the showman has to sit down, lick his pencil and laboriously plan his seasonal circuit. This entails writing for a *standing*, either to a private lessee who may be a Ride Master assembling his satellites, or to his own trade union The Showmen's Guild of Great Britain, who lease ground from corporations on behalf of their members. The chief co-ordinating factor between independent showmen is probably their trade newspaper *World's Fair*, which, even for the uninitiated, from week to week provides a fascinating insight into a world that few of us know much about.

So, on the modern fairground there are few random arrivals and everything is organised with the precision of a military manoeuvre. Everything—that is—except the weather.

As was previously explained, nowadays fairs cannot always expect to occupy the hard standing they originally had on market squares. More often than not they are moved to grass sites where if it is hot the ground turns to dust, if wet a quagmire. Either way these are conditions which radically affect the showmen. Good weather makes it easier for them to construct their amusements but tempts local citizens to seek other outdoor diversions—boating, swimming, seaside excursions and the rest. Adverse weather conditions may persuade patrons to brighten a wet day by a visit to the fair, but for the showmen causes a multitude of headaches.

Arriving overnight they must haul heavy tackle on to soft and frequently uneven ground and in a matter of hours present it in safe working order. The passage of lorries and trucks converging on this type of fairground causes it to liquefy and latecomers are bogged down and have to be manhandled or winched to their allotted positions.

A comparison which readily presents itself when describing the building up operation on the fairground, is that of giant do-it-yourself kits or jigsaws being rapidly assembled. Rides fit together by the simple arrangement of corresponding numbers and colours, so in theory, even unskilled and illiterate labour should be able to match compatible sections and get it right, but obviously it is the Ride Master, with his intimate knowledge of every moving part, who supervises the operation. He is also the one who meticulously organises the stacking of the dismantled machine so that on the next fairground each section is unloaded in logical sequence.

It is this exemplary attention to detail which makes travelling funfairs safe. The travelling showmen erect and dismantle their amusements almost every week of their working year. If anything is wrong they would know it in a moment and put it right. No showman makes money if his ride is out of commission! Although few and far between, serious accidents which have occurred on fairgrounds have invariably happened on fixed amusement sites where day-to-day maintenance is not such a personal matter.

When weather conditions on council sites are particularly bad, part of the rental agreement these days obligates the local authority to spread ashes and straw on the fairground mid-ways. However, this still doesn't prevent mud being carried on to the rides. Behind the scenes where the generators and living trailers are parked, conditions in wet weather can be even worse, families having to negotiate a sea of mud to attend to their amusements, fetch water from the communal tap or use their outdoor toilets. But regardless of weather conditions, the showmen maintain high standards of cleanliness. Rides are kept clean and no fairground child worth his salt would take his muddy boots into the family caravan, a structure which today is usually a very stylish affair.

Old-style living wagons were often home-made by the show-men. Utilising a solid wheeled flat truck as a base, they then constructed wagons which were largely of a traditional design. Outside the wagon was panelled and painted, usually maroon on the sides and cream on top and decorated with gold-leaf scroll-work. A stackpipe protruded through the roof, there were two horses in the shafts, curtains at the windows and underneath, between the wheels, the low-hung *belly box* for storing anything from pots and pans to live chickens. The interior was lined with polished mahogany inset with mirrors, had *angel lamp* paraffin lights and a range for cooking and heating.

The contemporary showman's spacious living van is custom built to luxurious specifications and, in many cases, luxuriously priced. One 40 feet long and 8 feet wide with underfloor central heating, leather lounge suite with cocktail cabinet, microwave oven and flush toilet is listed in *World's Fair* at a mere £20,000!

Constantly on the move from February to November, the travelling funfair people are at work providing amusements for others. Possibly for three months out of each year they disappear —rather like flies in wintertime— to their Winter Quarters. These are open yards situated up and down the countryside where they are permitted to park just long enough to overhaul their equipment ready for the coming season.

It is at the *back end* of the year that the showman's inherent craftsmanship can be most clearly demonstrated as he refurbishes his equipment, utilising the practical expertise he has learned from childhood when he was naturally apprenticed to his parents.

117

War time 3 ton truck,
still in use 1976

These are the skills he will pass down to his children, perpetuating an independent way of life which is not only traditional but able to intelligently adapt to the age in which it finds itself. This, if for no other reason, makes the travelling showman unique. Carpentry, engineering, driving, electrical wiring, straightforward painting and the intricate lettering and designs which typify his calling, are all within the self-taught capabilities of the ordinary showman. Only since determined officialdom has caught up with him has the modern showman learned to regret his lack of education.

Although, theoretically, fair-children were supposed to attend school whenever they arrived in a town or village, in practice they seldom did so. This wasn't entirely due to the showman's distaste for the conventional, but more the sheer physical discomfort suffered by a child geared to an outdoor lifestyle. Having to sit quietly within the claustrophobic walls of a building was in itself a sufficient deterrent to education but not the only one. Showmen's children also had to contend with the fact that they were always the newcomers in the classroom, had little in common with their *flatty* (house dwelling) classmates and because they were *different*, were also considered by the other children to be in some way inferior—an attitude of mistrust which hasn't always been confined to their schooldays. In addition to these drawbacks,

Living van. Once belonged to Shipley's Amusements. Now in farm yard, near York 1974

overworked teachers hardly felt it worthwhile expending energy on transient children. So, it isn't too difficult to appreciate the travelling showman's basic antipathy to education although many now have an entirely different viewpoint.

Modern showmen who can afford to do so send their children to exclusive boarding schools. During the holidays these children return to live on the fairground with their extended families and help as they've always done on candy-floss and Roll 'Em In stalls. It may take more than one generation of educated showmen to dilute the nomad blood in their veins but it does seem probable that the writing is already on the wagon wall.

In order to succeed, today's showman has to be both fearless impresario and astute businessman, confident enough to invest thousands of pounds in the latest computorised rides, mentally capable of fighting his way through the tangle of legislation devised to constrict every aspect of his working life from public safety on the Waltzer to hygiene on the brandy-snap stall.

Each year funfair people lose traditional fairground sites to urban redevelopment, and upon leaving their Winter Quarters in February can no longer be sure that they will be able to return there at the end of the season. But where else can they go?

Skilled beyond the average working man, the showman has no

Steam Yachts, built 1901 by Savages of Kings Lynn. These Yachts remain in original form except for an engine change. The Organ is a 46 key Chiappa. These Yachts are the only steam driven set left in current use, and are regular attenders at Hull Fair

indenture papers to prove it. Living in a mobile home which he is not allowed to park for more than a restricted period, he belongs to no established community, so cannot put his name down for a council house. The travelling showmen are true nomads, independent and proud of their birthright. Deprived of their traditional lifestyle—like the Dodo—they cannot exist.

Already wealthy showmen have financial interests in fixed amusement arcades whilst others divide their time between travelling fairs and semi-permanent concessions at holiday camps, seaside promenades, zoos and safari parks. For the rest of the travelling people perseverance is a poor combatant for inexorably rising costs and beaurocratic red tape more binding than the ribbons of old-time Maypoles! The future trend is towards permanent funfairs such as those at Blackpool, Great Yarmouth and Margate, mechanical playgrounds easily supervised by local authorities reluctant to organise the periodic comings and goings of itinerant entertainers. All the same, do the inhabitants of our steel and concrete jungles any longer care about the anachronistic pleasures of the travelling fairs? This is a debatable question.

Remember Harry Lee and his old-time Steam Yachts? In 1960 after ten years of scarcely making ends meet, Harry Lee took his ride to the first Steam Rally, held at White Waltham in Berkshire. It attracted record crowds eager to see a working display of old fairground organs playing perforated paper music, steam traction engines polluting the air with black smoke and a handful of fairground rides from the 1900s which had somehow survived. Only Harry Lee was operating his ride in its original state which he has continued to do to this day, now a much sought-after attraction both at the increasingly popular Steam Fairs and on the traditional fairgrounds.

There will always be those who lament the changing face of the fair and turn nostalgically to preservation societies to safeguard the diminishing remnants of bygone merry-making. Meantime the vital textures of the travelling funfair slip away.

Fairs and revels, highdays and holidays, every citizen still has the right to enjoy these simple pleasures—just so long as he can appreciate that behind the incredible gyrations of the latest speed machine, the amplified pop music, the hot-dog and candy-floss stalls, on his own front doorstep exists a living, breathing example of the medieval past.

Acknowledgements

The publishers wish to express their gratitude to the Kunsthistorisches Museum, Vienna, for the illustration on the jacket *Peasant Dance* by Brueghel (c. 1525/30–1569), also *Flemish Fair* by Pieter Brueghel (The Younger, 1564-1637). To Malcolm Slater of Huntington, York, for photographs of Fairgrounds, Steam Engines, Rides, Wagons and Trailers. To World's Fair and Mr F. Mellor for helpful advice and loan of photographs.

Bibliography

ABRAM, A. *Social Life in the Fifteenth Century* 1909.

ADDISON, W. *English Fairs and Markets* 1953.

ADDY, S. O. *Church and Manor* 1913.

ANDREWS, W. *Bygone England* 1892.

    Famous Frosts and Frost Fairs 1887.

BRETT, H. *English Myths and Traditions* 1952.

BRYANT, ARTHUR *England in the Reign of Charles II* 1934.

CHRISTIAN, ROY *Old English Customs,* The Country Life Book of 1966.

COULTON, G. G. *Social Life in Britain from the Conquest*
    to the Reformation 1918.

    Life in the Middle Ages 1930.

CUTTS, E. L. *Scenes and Characters of the Middle Ages* 1926.

DYER, T. THISTLETON. *British Popular Customs* 1876.

GOMME, A. B. *Traditional Games of England, Scotland and Ireland* 1894–8.

GOMME, G. L. *The Village Community* 1890.

HARRISON, WILLIAM *A Description of England* 1577.

HOLE, CHRISTINA *English Sports and Pastimes* 1949.

    English Custom and Usage 1941.

HONE, WILLIAM *The Every-day Book*   Vols I and II 1825–27.

    The Table Book 1827.

    The Year Book 1832.

JAMES, E. O. *Seasonal Feasts and Festivals* 1961.

JUSSERAND, J. J. *Wayfaring Life in the Middle Ages* 1899.

LECKY, W. E. H. *The History of England in the Eighteenth Century* 1883.

LENNARD, R (Editor). *Englishmen at Rest and Play* 1931.

MORLEY, H. T. *Memoirs of Bartholomew Fair* 1859.

MUNCEY, R. W. L. *Old English Fairs* 1936.

PASTON, G. *Sidelights on the Georgian Period* 1902.

PORTEUS, C. *The Beauty and Mystery of Well Dressing* 1949.

SALZMAN, L. F. *English Life in The Middle Ages* 1926.

    England in Tudor Times 1953.

SHARMAN, W. *Old Fairs of Northampton* 1903.

SNELL, F. J. *The Customs of Old England* 1911.

STRUTT, JOSEPH *Sports and Pastimes of the People of England* 1801
    (Edited by William Hone, 1867).

TRAIL, H. D. *Social England* 1895.

TREVELYN, G. M. *English Social History* 1944.

WALFORD, C. *Fairs, Past and Present* 1883.

WARD, NED *The London Spy* 1698–1703 (Edited by A. L. Hayward,
    1927).

WHISTLER, L. *The English Festivals* 1947.

WYKES, ALAN *Gambling* 1964.

Index

Illustrations are indicated by numbers in italics

126

127